# MIDLAND

# MIDLAND

## REPORTS FROM FLYOVER COUNTRY

**Michael Croley and Jack Shuler, eds.**

TILLER PRESS

New York   London   Toronto   Sydney   New Delhi

TILLER PRESS

An Imprint of Simon & Schuster, Inc.
1230 Avenue of the Americas
New York, NY 10020

First Tiller Press trade paperback edition September 2020

TILLER PRESS and colophon are trademarks of Simon & Schuster, Inc.

For information about special discounts for bulk purchases, please contact Simon & Schuster Special Sales at 1-866-506-1949 or business@simonandschuster.com.

The Simon & Schuster Speakers Bureau can bring authors to your live event. For more information or to book an event, contact the Simon & Schuster Speakers Bureau at 1-866-248-3049 or visit our website at www.simonspeakers.com.

Interior design by Laura Levatino

Manufactured in the United States of America

1   3   5   7   9   10   8   6   4   2

Library of Congress Cataloging-in-Publication Data

Names: Croley, Michael, author. | Shuler, Jack, author.
Title: Midland : reports from flyover country / [edited by] Michael Croley & Jack Shuler.
Description: Reports from flyover country | New York : Tiller Press, 2020.
Identifiers: LCCN 2020021315 (print) | LCCN 2020021316 (ebook) | ISBN 9781982147778 (paperback) | ISBN 9781982147785 (ebook)
Classification: LCC E913.3 .M53 2020  (print) | LCC E913.3 (ebook) | DDC 977--dc23
LC record available at https://lccn.loc.gov/2020021315
LC ebook record available at https://lccn.loc.gov/2020021316

ISBN 978-1-9821-4777-8
ISBN 978-1-9821-4778-5 (ebook)

*This book is dedicated to the journalists and writers covering the cities and towns—the communities they live in— far too often overlooked in our national coverage.*

*We thank you.*

# CONTENTS

## Campaign Trails

Contents

## Constituent Concerns

# Contents

## Solutions

# Contents

## Afterword

# MIDLAND

# FOREWORD

## Connie Schultz

IN THE SUMMER BEFORE the 2004 presidential election, *The Plain Dealer* published a deeply reported series titled "The Five Ohios." It was conceived as a response—perhaps rebuke is a better word—to decades of journalism by people who don't live here presuming to tell the stories of the eleven million people who do. It could have been subtitled "We've Had It Up to Here."

By 2004, Ohio had picked the winner in every presidential election except two for the previous 104 years. Once again, we were the landing pad for national political reporters swooping in for a quick stereotype or two. You can find someone to say something stupid on any corner in America, and Ohio becomes the promised land for that nonsense every four years. Rent a car, eat in a diner, and find five people to confirm your worst assumptions about us. File the story and off you go. Don't forget to mention how folksy we are.

The problem with this coverage, in Ohio and across the Midwest, is that it's a collage of snapshots rather than a mirror that reflects the complex alignments and vulnerabilities unique to each state.

In 2004, for example, part of Ohio was the industrial heartland. Another part was the farm belt, and yet another was Appalachian. In the southwest corner, southern accents and Republicans were prevalent, while in central Ohio, Columbus was already becoming the largest city in the state, and becoming more liberal because of those who were moving there.

Try illustrating that rich diversity of a Midwestern state with a day's worth of interviews in a town of your choice. You may laugh, but plenty of reporters did just that.

As a columnist at *The Plain Dealer* in 2004, I appreciated the hard work of my colleagues, but I wasn't surprised by their findings. I grew up in small-town Ashtabula, about an hour's drive east of Cleveland on Interstate 90. When I was younger, I used to joke to people that it was a town you passed on your way to somewhere else. I don't say that anymore because the people of my roots don't deserve to be a punchline. We were a racially diverse, working-class town where a lot of union families could afford to dream big for their kids.

I was the first in my working-class family to go to college, so I learned all about Midwestern stereotypes, one ignorant question at a time. In every year of elementary school, half of my classmates were black. To this day, I can state that single fact and watch the mouths of educated white people fall open like a Lake Erie perch. When I was younger, that reaction used to offend me. Now it's a hobby. The only way we break down false narratives about our part of the country is to tell our stories, one cliché-crashing tale at a time.

To do this, we must wrestle the narrative away from people who think we're all just what's-the-matter-with-Kansas. That's why this diverse collection of essays is so important. *Midland: Reports from Flyover Country* doesn't just challenge stereotypes about this part of the country; it grabs you by the shirt collar and yanks you into the world as we know it. The view is beautiful, and often heartbreaking. These writers have not forgotten the people of their roots, but they also don't pretty them up for public consumption. We are messy and complicated, and built layer by layer. Peel those layers back, and you get to the heart of who we are.

A good book surprises you, even catches you off guard, and that was surely true for me as I read these stories, even though I've lived in the Midwest all of my life. You think you know yourself, but then you find out there are entire parts of your story you've yet to discover. I wish I could share a quote or two from every essay in this book. Instead, I'll mention just one, Bryan Mealer's "Can't We All Just Get Along? A Road Trip with My Trump-Loving Cousin," because it captures the essence of what this book sets out to do. Life will surprise you, time and again. I started out not wanting to read Bryan's essay—Trump? No, thanks—and now, weeks later, I'm still thinking about it.

Frances loves Donald Trump and Bryan doesn't. In the second sentence, we find out Frances has made a crude comment about immigrants. "Why," I said out loud, "does he want to spend any time with this woman?"

The answer comes in layers.

She's his cousin.

I sigh and nod.

We've got those in my family, too, including my late brother, a proud Trump supporter even after he lost his job, his car, and his home. Some of my friends, after hearing my account of yet another frustrating conversation with him, would demand to know why I even bothered. My answer was always the same: He was my baby brother, and I loved him before he loved Trump.

Bryan's humanity, and his innate curiosity about his cousin, allows him, and us, to see the layers that built Frances, from the broken dreams of her childhood to the unfulfilled promises of her life as a young woman. She pokes and prods him, seemingly eager to ignite their differences, but he remains calm and stays curious as they drive toward the White House for an event where Frances hopes to shake the president's hand. Bryan has a plan.

Along the way, Frances has to meet various groups of people she thought were her collective enemy until they start talking to one another. She is a captive audience in the car as Bryan launches debates about Christianity, LBGTQ rights, Black Lives Matter, and guns, for starters.

It's the fraught Thanksgiving dinner, spread over miles.

Why do we bother?

The answers are in the layers, peeled back one essay at a time by those who know how to separate fact from fiction, and relish the endeavor. The best answers come from answering the right questions, but that's only part of it. You have to listen, and with an open heart. You may not like everyone you meet in these stories, but you'll be wiser for having known them. The real them, free of the stereotypes that are as incomplete as they are convenient. That's when the real conversation can begin.

# INTRODUCTION

**A LITTLE LESS THAN FOUR YEARS AGO,** we thought America might be on the verge of meaningful change. Lasting change. Of course, as it turns out, we were right, but not in the way we envisioned. We don't know yet whether the changes wrought by Donald Trump's presidency will be lasting. But one thing that wasn't surprising, that historic night in November 2016, was the rapidly developing narrative around rural voters. Call them middle class. Call them lower middle class, even. But for many people in communities across this country, even those living at points firmly between Los Angeles and New York, their anger and frustration began to be directed toward "flyover country." The uneducated middle. A large swath of this nation's population feels that another large swath continues to vote against their economic interest.

As two southerners who grew up in racially charged towns far removed from the mainstream media, we know that it's easy to grasp at stereotypes and generalizations as we try to make sense of the world today. But we also know, personally, that these "middle" areas are complicated. To wit, we are also professors at a small liberal arts college in central Ohio, surrounded by once-thriving towns, once-thriving family farms, and too many people whose lives have been hollowed out in the last forty years by unchecked capitalism and globalization. This back-drop foretold a story that the polls didn't. From Columbus to Cleveland, if you traveled Ohio 13, you would have seen that nearly every farm and every house was pro-Trump. In the small college town where we live and work, the houses alternated their allegiances. It may not be the most scientific measurement, but it ultimately proved more illuminating than the pie charts from the pundits.

Which is to say: we were not surprised by Trump's election. Our neighbors told us—and showed us—what could happen. You can't boil one group down to anything, but in the wake of Trump's victory, the Trump Country narrative took hold. The blame was placed squarely on rural communities that are routinely forgotten by the very media now doing the finger-pointing. It did not matter that exit polls showed Clinton won working-class voters but lost college-educated women. Trump and his "strength" and his "tough talk" clearly spoke to the little guy, went the narrative.

We all know this now, of course. The writers in this collection knew it then, back in 2015 and early 2016. They knew because they live and work in "Trump Country." They have abandoned the media capitals to pursue careers and raise their families in the towns and states they love, that feel like home. They're interested in getting it right, not because of a journalistic creed, but because they want to show the rest of the country that the struggles of life matter there just as much as anywhere else. And unlike the parachute reporter from one of the two coasts, they have to face their subjects the next day at the grocery store, at the coffee shop, picking the kids up from school.

There has never been a more crucial time for the journalism we seek to highlight in this collection. As our media giants falter and fracture, as our ability to disseminate truth and facts gets drowned out by the compulsive electronic bird call of our president, the stories in this book remind us that elections matter, yes, but also that life still persists and that the human struggle to make meaning of our lives is universal.

## HOW THIS BOOK CAME ABOUT

After the election, writer Ted Genoways put out a call—and a challenge, of sorts—on Facebook, to the writers he knew in the Midwest. He asked them to keep reporting, keeping in mind the narrative that was already unfolding about their communities. We were among those listed, and that was the first step toward the book you're holding. Quickly, Ted's thread moved from the virtual to an actual event known as the Between Coasts Forums. It first convened in January 2017. Fifty writers from around the Midwest (and a few from the coasts, too) met to discuss how to subvert a mainstream narrative that seemed false from our vantage points, and to discuss the challenges that would pose under an administration that, from its very first day, was routinely lying to the American people.

Those forums have become a sort of professional development conference for us, though less about being seen than about getting to work. A Midwestern ethos pervades, if you like. As the caretakers of the forums, we want to ensure that people who cover underreported communities and places in the middle have a place to gather and to be heard. Esther Honig, a former NPR reporter turned long-form freelancer whose work is featured here, remarked at a recent forum (number five!) in Lincoln, Nebraska, that the reason she feels committed to this group of journalists is that we make it seem cool to not move to New York, Los Angeles, or Washington, D.C. That pretty much sums it up.

At the forums, our students and local documentary filmmakers rub elbows with seasoned journalists like *The New Yorker*'s Peter Slevin, whose piece on Bernie Sanders and socialism in Wisconsin runs alongside our former student Fitale Wari's excellent essay on feeling afraid as an African American woman during the Trump presidency. Heather Sinclair Shaw's piece on a prodigal daughter returning and surprising herself with a run for mayor appears next to Ted Genoways's own piece about strange bedfellows: environmental activists and white nationalists working side by side in Freemont, Nebraska, to stop a Costco chicken processing plant from opening.

The goal of this book is not just to highlight the excellent reporting by excellent writers that has already appeared in print but, like our forums, to give space and voice to writers whose work has not gained the purchase and audience it deserves. Ultimately, we hope you'll see that the breadth, talent, and diversity of the Midwest spreads as far as the cornfields, and that the worst thing we could do in this political moment is misjudge or neglect the stories that reside there. Instead, let's stop to walk around these neighborhoods, to consider their fates along with our own. Their stories are your stories. Their country is ours.

# Campaign Trails

# DOWN RIVER

## Mei-Ling Hopgood

hen I was a kid, my hometown of Taylor, Michigan, sat on one of the lowest rungs of the suburban Detroit social hierarchy. We were Down River, southwest of the D, just east of Metro Airport. Outsiders called us (mostly white) trash; we lived in public housing and trailer parks near railroad tracks.

"You come from Taylortucky," laughed a scuba instructor I met while traveling in Hawaii. Whenever people ripped us, I liked to think I knew my town so much better than they did.

It was true that generations of poor southern families migrated north in search of jobs at auto plants, settling in Taylor and the surrounding Down River communities. Indeed, back in the 1980s, when I was in middle and high school, we were a burnout-friendly kind of place, and proud of it. At the Get and Go across the street from my high school, teens lingered to smoke. In college, we'd use fake IDs to dance in windowless saloons on weedy lots.

I was always aware of how different I was in Down River. My parents were, in fact, white-collar. My dad, who grew up in Taylor, was president of the Michigan Federation of Teachers, and my mother was an elementary school principal. My childhood friends thought we were rich because my father designed and built our house, which sat on two acres of woods.

Some differences were more painful, and back then, I didn't talk about them much. Taylor's population then was mostly white, and about 4 percent black. My parents adopted me from Taiwan and my younger brothers from Korea, and I used to joke that we made up three-fourths of the 1 percent Asians in our city. Once people met my brothers and me, they remembered us, for better or worse. My teachers always recalled our faces, names, and how well we did in school. My ear was tuned to the hisses of "ching, chang, chung," and screams of "Go back to China!" from rusting Ford Mustangs. The signs outside the United Auto Workers parking lots read "Made in the USA Only." The signs—and the people who put them up—were talking about cars. But sometimes I wondered if they wanted to keep people like me out.

Over time I have come to believe being raised in a gritty place like Taylor made me tougher and more resilient. Many more people showed me love than hate.

My life there was the springboard from which I leapt into the world, ending up in places as far-flung as Argentina and Taiwan. Great math teachers helped me ace calculus, and my journalism teacher helped me shape a career. I was valedictorian and class president. And union scholarships helped me pay my way through college. Friends from high school eagerly celebrated my success as a writer.

But the thing about racism is that it bleeds onto and stains everything it touches. Those marks change the fabric of who you are and how you view the world, even when you think you have moved on.

When I worked as a reporter for the *Detroit Free Press* in the 1990s, I lived in Troy, Royal Oak, Ann Arbor—communities where people seemed smarter, richer, and slightly more diverse. Yet people still made fun of

4

where I was from. I lived in different states and countries; built a life, learned languages, evolved how I felt about race, culture, and identity.

Meanwhile, Taylor changed. Most of the people I hung out with moved away. The population dropped from almost 78,000 when I was in high school to an estimated 61,000 in 2019, according to the census. The city's leaders—including my father, who passed away in 2002—built a more economically diverse city, a nice golf course, and small, new clusters of modern homes on once-vacant lots. Today, the city is 72 percent white, 17 percent black, 5 percent Hispanic, and 2 percent Asian.

When my brother ran for Michigan state representative in the 22nd District in 2002, we wondered whether he would use his real name in his campaign. Could a place like Taylor and neighboring Romulus vote for a guy with a Korean name like Hoon-Yung? He went door-to-door, making his case. In the end, he won, and in 2010 was elected state senator, leaving Lansing only when he was term-limited out.

I was relieved that my town had proved me wrong. I also realized that my own adolescent scars still shaped my perception of Taylor. But as it turns out, the people there really could look at Hoon's accomplishments and platform instead of his race.

My old assumptions reared their head again when my mom told me, during the run-up to the presidential election of 2016, that people in my hometown of Taylor, Michigan, were going for Trump.

"I'm afraid to put up a Hillary sign," she told me. Once upon a time, my parents filled their front yard with neon political signs during election season. But now she feared someone might vandalize her home.

I was surprised at first. I had known our Detroit suburb as a Democratic stronghold, a hard-core union town where people made and bought cars from General Motors and Ford, and voted a straight blue ticket. Then, it occurred to me that Taylor might, in fact, be just the kind of place that would turn to Donald Trump—for those same reasons.

I'd been gritting my teeth as I read my social media feed. I had vowed not to defriend people for views that contrasted with my own. But the discourse—Trump and his supporters' references to immigrants as criminals, to people of color as irresponsible—struck at the heart of my deepest sensitivities. I'd spent my childhood fearing people thought these things of me, that behind their smiles they judged me as un-American. I filtered others' political beliefs through my own pain.

Truth be told, in the years before 2016, I paid scant attention to the politics of my home state, let alone Taylor. But on Election Day, I watched as Trump's percentage of the vote crept upward in many states, including Michigan, and knew he was headed for victory. I watched as Wayne County teetered from Clinton to Trump and was floored. The city of Detroit would eventually turn the county in Clinton's favor, but Trump won Michigan by just more than 10,000 votes. The state was key to Trump's presidency.

I was devastated. And I did exactly what I had sworn I wouldn't do. I lashed out against one of my sweetest friends from my high school days. During those brutal teenage years, Faith had been loving and supportive while others were cruel. She was soft-spoken, always concerned with how you were, patient and kind. But online, she had led an open charge to rally suburban women for Trump, denying accusations of racism. We had not talked in years. In a state of mourning, my one act of retaliation was to defriend Faith.

In that moment, I believed that Trump won in Taylor because Taylor was racist, and therefore anyone who voted for Trump had to be as well.

Since then, I like to think I've made my way back to the belief that most people are more complex than their political views. When I looked at Wayne County's election results, I saw that even though Trump won in 21 out of 31 precincts in Taylor, Clinton won overall. Whenever I've posted, during indignant moments, memories of childhood racism, I receive a wash of sympathy from old friends from Taylor.

We had no idea, they say. We are sorry.

How could you not know? I wonder. But during these times, it is easy to cast people in simple terms—even the people you once knew or currently know well. As a journalist, I try to challenge myself to speak in specifics, not to draw generalizations or tar a group for the behavior of an individual. I tell my students at Northwestern University, who tend to be a liberal lot, that during challenging times, we are forced to reexamine what we believe and who we are. I ask them to lean into the things that make them uncomfortable. I like to think I, personally, have leaned away from, or disproved, the stereotypes imposed on me. I have not always done the same for my hometown, the friends who grew up there, and the people who live there now.

I finally looked at Faith's public Facebook feed the other day. I noticed that one of the posts I can still see is one celebrating the release of my first book a decade ago, at my launch party. I immediately felt embarrassed for jumping to conclusions, without reaching out, asking her why.

I did not try to understand her journey and who she had become.

Still, calling her would mean I would have to confront regret—for labeling, for lashing out, and for losing touch with people who were once dear to me. I've not yet found the energy to reach out. I still like to think I will.

# THE MANY, TANGLED AMERICAN DEFINITIONS OF SOCIALISM

### Peter Slevin

As Donald Trump declares that "America will never be a social-ist country" and Democratic presidential candidates struggle to put a name to their progressive policies, the historian John Gurda would like to add some perspective to how we think about socialism. The term has been "ground into the dust over the years," he told me, when we met in his hometown of Milwaukee, and his aim is to rehabilitate it. "Part of my self-assigned role is to provide some of the context, the nuance, where it makes sense again. Because it's the straw man, it's the boogeyman for an awful lot of people."

Last year, when the Democratic National Committee chose Mil-waukee to host its 2020 convention, the executive director of Wisconsin's Republican Party mocked the decision, noting that, in the twentieth cen-tury, Milwaukee, alone among American cities, had elected three socialist mayors. "With the rise of Bernie Sanders and the embrace of socialism by its newest leaders, the American left has come full circle," Mark Jefferson, the head of the party, said. But Gurda, who is seventy-two and has spent nearly all of his years in Milwaukee, thinks that the socialism practiced there deserves another look. The record, he said, reveals a "movement calling itself socialist that governed well, that governed frugally, that governed creatively, that served the broader common interest. We abandon that vision at our peril. All this fearmongering about nationalizing industries and taking from the rich—the Robin Hood thing—that's a gross misrepresentation."

Senator Bernie Sanders, the only avowed socialist in the presidential race, delivered a speech in June of 2019 that presented his brand of democratic socialism as an unthreatening egalitarianism, in the spirit of Franklin D. Roosevelt and Martin Luther King Jr. He called it "the unfinished business of the New Deal" and recited an "economic bill of rights" that included the right to a living wage, health care, a secure retirement, and a clean environment. "'Socialism,'" Sanders quoted President Harry Truman as saying, in 1952, "'is the epithet they have hurled at every advance that people have made in the last twenty years. Socialism is what they called Social Security. Socialism is what they called farm-price supports. Socialism is what they called bank-deposit insurance. Socialism is what they called the growth of free and independent labor. Socialism is their name for almost everything that helps all of the people.'"

More than sixty years after Truman spoke those words, socialism still is marked by strong connotations and conflicting definitions in the United States. For decades, many Americans defined it in terms of the Cold War, equating the term with state control of the economy and, more often than not, authoritarian rule. Sanders, who first ran for Vermont governor forty-seven years ago, has found a following among a new generation that is not steeped in Cold War ideology. The movement, personified by Representative Alexandria Ocasio-Cortez, is trying to chart a path away from a new Gilded Age of garish inequality and rising economic anxiety. In recent weeks, as I spoke with dozens of voters and political figures in

Wisconsin, it was clear from our conversations that the term conjures dramatically different images, from decency to social decay. Some equate socialism with a fair-minded social contract largely underwritten by a market economy, while others think of Stalin's Soviet Union—or, more recently, Venezuela, where the late Hugo Chávez and the current leader, Nicolás Maduro, ran a prospering economy into the ground under socialism's banner. As Democrats try to regain Wisconsin and other swing states that they narrowly lost to Trump in 2016, candidates are eager to redefine the party as responsive to the needs of working-class people, and Republicans are all too eager to hang a negative label on them.

"Understanding this word is going to be a significant part of the 2020 landscape," Patrick Murray, the director of the Monmouth University poll, said, adding, "It's going to be messy." As he tries to get to the bottom of voters' understanding of socialism, he's finding a series of contradictions. A Monmouth survey published in May found that only 29 percent of Americans consider socialism compatible with American values, yet 50 percent believe socialism is "a way to make things fairer for working people."[1]

A Gallup survey, released in May, found that 51 percent of Americans believe that socialism would be a "bad thing" for the country, while 43 percent consider it a "good thing."[2] Putting it diplomatically, Gallup's Mohamed Younis noted that American understandings of the term are "nuanced and multifaceted." In a poll last year, Gallup asked what socialism means. The answers were all over the map. The most common responses, at 23 percent, fell into the category of "no opinion" or "equal standing for everybody, all equal in rights, equal in distribution." The next most common answer, at 17 percent, was "government ownership or control." Then there were the 6 percent who thought socialism meant "talking to people, being social, social media."[3]

In the confusion over meanings, Trump and the Republicans see an opportunity to define the terms of the 2020 election, with socialism serving as epithet and warning. Warming up a crowd of more than ten thousand supporters near Green Bay on April 27, Trump's campaign manager, Brad Parscale, said that the president would be running against "a bunch of crazy socialists."[4] In late May, the Republican National Committee and the Trump presidential campaign sent an email to supporters calling on them as "Patriotic Americans" to sign an "Official Reject Socialism Petition." "America was founded on liberty and independence—not government coercion, domination and control," it read. "We are born free and we will stay free. Stand with President Trump to tell Democrats that America will NEVER be a socialist country!"

Gurda, the historian, likens the Republican tactics to the Red-baiting first used against Milwaukee socialists more than a century ago and perfected in the 1950s by Wisconsin's own Senator Joseph McCarthy, who later was censured by the Senate for his unscrupulous ways.[5] The city had three socialist mayors: Emil Seidel, who served two years, starting in 1910; Daniel Hoan, in office from 1916 to 1940; and Frank Zeidler, who served three terms between 1948 and 1960. They were known for clean government, solid budgeting, a focus on public health, including vaccination campaigns and improved sewerage, as well as stronger safety standards in the city's workplaces and hiring practices that valued merit over connections. More evolutionary than revolutionary, they avoided what Gurda called the "dense ideological thickets that waylaid other leftists." Garden Homes, completed in 1923, was the first municipally sponsored public-housing project in the country. A key to their popularity was their ability to persuade voters that government was "a coöperative us," Gurda said, not "a predatory them."

"The word 'public' is used again and again and again and again," Gurda told me as we sat at a weathered picnic table beside Lake Michigan, near Bradford Beach. "Public parks, which is why I had you meet me here. Public libraries, public schools, a public port, public housing. The term Frank Zeidler used all the time was 'public enterprise.' It's important to underline 'enterprise,' because they were as creative as any capitalist, and as aggressive as any capitalist, in trying to create a system that worked for the common man and woman." He added, "They were not tax-and-spend. The city actually, for a time, had no debt. They were frugal."

The city's socialist history has its roots in Europe. The failure of the revolutions of 1848 triggered an exodus of German intellectuals and reformers who made their way to Wisconsin shortly after it became the thirtieth state. The newcomers opposed autocracy, repression, and the excesses of monarchs and plutocrats, and yet they were more evolutionary than revolutionary, a trait their successors would share. Central to their influence in the late 1800s and early 1900s was the rise of labor unions that fought to improve factory conditions. "There was no OSHA, there was no health insurance, there was no workers' comp. The cards were all on the side of the employer," Gurda said. A strike for an eight-hour day, however, led to bloodshed in May 1886 when a state militia summoned by the governor opened fire on fifteen hundred marching workers, killing seven people.[6] The strike failed, but incensed workers and their supporters formed a political party that swept into power quickly, if briefly.

It was ten years into the new century, in 1910, that Milwaukee elected Seidel as its first socialist mayor. A patternmaker by trade, he was derided by ideological purists as a "Sewer Socialist" for building what would now be called infrastructure. Looking back on his tenure in the 1930s, he offered a response to the critics, whom he nicknamed "Eastern smarties."

"Yes, we wanted sewers in the workers' houses," Seidel wrote. "But we wanted much, oh, so very much more than sewers. We wanted our workers to have pure air; we wanted them to have sunshine; we wanted planned homes; we wanted living wages; we wanted recreation for young and old; we wanted vocational education; we wanted a chance for every human being to be strong and live a life of happiness."[7] To make that happen, Seidel said, he and his allies sought to deliver parks and playgrounds, swimming pools and beaches, reading rooms and "clean fun." He called the effort the "Milwaukee Social Democratic movement."

When Gurda compares the present-day reformers who call themselves democratic socialists to the Milwaukee socialists of generations past, he sees different issues, but "the same impulse: the glaring disparities of American life." These are the origins of his own mission, too, as he watches what he calls "the drift of society." Gurda says he is not a socialist nor a Sanders supporter, and yet it bothers him that Republican critics "identify socialism as whatever they care to, while the reality of what it was, especially at the municipal level, is not even forgotten, just completely ignored." Meanwhile, as GOP spitballs rain down, Democrats who favor such policies as Medicare for All, free college tuition, and an ambitious, government-powered climate-change agenda called the Green New Deal are laboring to figure out how to deal with the term.

The former Colorado governor John Hickenlooper, barely registering in the polls so far, is warning Democrats to steer clear. On June 1, he told the California Democratic Convention, "If we want to beat Donald Trump and achieve big, progressive goals, socialism is not the answer." As the audience booed, he said, "You know, if we're not careful, we're going to end up helping to re-elect the worst President in American history."

Representative Ron Kind, a centrist Democrat who has represented a largely rural western Wisconsin district since 1997, sounded a similar alarm when I asked what sort of Democrat can win Wisconsin following Trump's 2016 victory. Kind favors a pragmatic, nonideological nominee who "isn't pressing buttons to polarize both sides." As a matter of tactics, he told me, "it would be a mistake to fall into the socialism trap" set by Republicans. In fact, Kind said, Trump is the candidate who favors state intervention in the economy in ways most commonly associated with hard-line socialism. He described the president's approach as "authoritarian socialism" and said that the president's supporters "apparently don't recognize it when they see it."

That's the thing. There are no agreed-upon definitions of socialism—and any attempt at annotation risks proving the old campaign adage that if you're explaining, you're losing. "People don't vote on objective definitions. They vote on their visceral reaction to what they think the term means," Murray, the Monmouth poll director, said. He sees a divide by age and political party. In the survey released in May, only 6 percent of young Democrats and Independents who lean Democratic expressed negative feelings about socialism, while 76 percent of self-identified Republicans did.[8] As time goes on, Murray predicted, "We're probably going to continue seeing the negative use of 'socialism' in a political context lose its power."

Frank Luntz, a longtime Republican wordsmith, focus group leader, and strategist renowned for wrapping ideas into phrases that resonate with voters, offered an unlikely endorsement of that view. As he likes to tell his clients, who have included Newt Gingrich, Pat Buchanan, Ross Perot, and Rudy Giuliani, "It's not what you say, it's what they hear." Luntz had recently attended a Sanders rally in California when I asked him how socialism is playing in the campaign. "It's no longer the buzzkill it used to be," he said. "This is the first election cycle, at least in my lifetime, when I think it's possible that Democrats will nominate someone who prefers socialism to capitalism."

What Luntz hears from voters is something different from ten or twenty years ago. As a believer in what he calls "economic freedom," it worries him. "I believe the public is moving away from capitalism and toward socialism, and I've measured it. I see it, I hear it in my focus groups," he said. More and more people believe that the wealthy have rigged the system, and they want to unrig it. That makes more voters open to a disruptive figure like Trump and to candidates who promise a fairer deal through socialism. Luntz said that his message to "every CEO I can meet with, every business group that will listen, and politicians from both political parties" is that they should take the popular sentiment seriously. The

Republican strategy of demonizing Democrats by likening their policies to Venezuela's is a mistake. "Just making up accusations won't work," he said, "not now, not when everyone knows the level of wealth inequality in the country."

It's no focus group, but in a series of interviews in Wisconsin in April and May, I saw the divide, and the confusion, over the meaning of socialism. It's about "sharing the wealth, but not taking away from others," Liz Rodman, a pharmacist from Missouri who was finishing her residency in Milwaukee, said. It means "looking at the greater good," her friend and fellow pharmacist Marshall Johnson said. Yet Kenneth O'Neill, who manages an appliance store, said that socialism would strip away individual rights. "Look what's happening in New York. You can't even supersize your sodas because they think we're too stupid to make our own choices."

On Memorial Day, I went to Milwaukee's Wood National Cemetery, where several hundred veterans and their families stood or sat in folding chairs, a few in wheelchairs, as dignitaries spoke of fallen warriors. As the crowd dispersed, Randy Zemel, who served in the Marines in Vietnam, considered the question of socialism. At seventy-four, he works with special education students, and still wears his metal Marine Corps dog tags around his neck. "Socialism's not the answer. It takes away the American spirit of working for something," he said, and he offered an example. "If I gave you a brand-new Corvette, free, you don't owe me a penny. I wonder what you'd think of that Corvette. You didn't work one second for it. Socialism is government giving it to you, so you squander it."

A few hours later and a few miles away, O'Neill and his wife, Darlene, waited for the parade to pass by. They are Trump fans, and they believe him when he says that the United States commands fresh respect in the world. When it comes to economic systems, they see no overlap between socialism and capitalism. "Socialism stagnates a country. Who wants to work for nothing? I'm all for capitalism. It weeds out what doesn't work," O'Neill said. He sees the Democratic Party heading down a dangerous road. House Speaker Nancy Pelosi, he said, "is trying her hardest to keep it out of the hands of the socialists, and I think she's losing."

Chris Sadowski, a corporate travel consultant, was also waiting for the parade to start, standing beneath an overhang in his yellow rain gear, with his Harley-Davidson lined up beside dozens of others. A lifelong Milwaukee resident whose father was a city worker and whose mother stitched leather seats for a company that supplied Harley-Davidson, he is frustrated by the demonization of socialism. "We've got to talk about the common good. When you have greed, no one comes out a winner except those on top," Sadowski said. He is no Trump fan, but he also thinks Democrats need to tread carefully when it comes to socialism, focusing on policies rather than labels. "Find other ways to talk about it," he advised. "People hear certain words and they shut down completely."

# SEARCHING FOR THE OTHER MIDWESTERN SWING VOTER

## (Spoiler: She's Black and Lives in Detroit)

### Wendy S. Walters

For two evenings in late July 2019, the 2020 Democratic presidential candidates debated at Detroit's Fox Theater, often invoking appeals to a mythical Midwestern voter through their proclamations of values and lamentations on the loss of manufacturing jobs.

Just a mile away from the theater, dozens of Detroiters gathered at McShane's Bar in a neighborhood called Corktown for a viewing party hosted by the nonpartisan coalition CitizenDetroit. A lively, mixed crowd paused to listen to each of the candidates' responses before scoffing, erupting in applause, or throwing out follow-up questions that would never be answered. Here were some of those "real" Midwestern voters—active, concerned, skeptical, and invested. Gazing around the room, I wondered whether the candidates truly understood who the Midwestern voter really is. After all, there were more Black women in the room than any other demographic group.

"Detroit is one of the most American cities that I can think of," says Candice Fortman, a lifelong Detroiter and media executive. "It is deeply rooted in this idea of democracy and freedom and hard work and unionizing, all things that are very American values. And, so, just because the people who live here don't fit the demographic makeup of what people like to believe this country is, makes it no less Midwestern and no less American."

The bias against Detroit's Midwestern status is twofold: It is a city that is 80 percent Black. Perhaps even more important—and most often ignored—is that more than 40 percent of homes have Black women as the head of household, with some estimates placing the number much higher.[1] In surrounding Wayne County, that figure remains around 29 percent.[2]

That so many Black women in Detroit are the primary wage earners, as well as the principal caretakers of children and parents, throws into stark relief how out of touch nostalgic depictions of auto industry patriarchs are with the actual profile of working people in the urban Midwest.

THOUGH UNION STRIKES and factory closings across the state were common during the late 1980s and early 1990s—when I was growing up there—I wanted to see if the solemnity surrounding this plant's closing struck a new chord. I drove over to the soon-to-be-shuttered Warren Transmission facility at Mound and Nine Mile roads the day before it was scheduled to close. Ostensibly, this plant is located in "Trump Country," as 53.6 percent of Macomb County voters chose the Republican candidate in the 2016 presidential election. Yet it's also just one mile north of Detroit, which is majority blue.

In the early afternoon on the day before the plant's final shifts, four flags flew under a blue sky: a U.S. flag, a GM flag, the UAW flag, and a POW/MIA flag. A handful of people carrying bags and boxes exited to assembly area F in the early afternoon. Earlier that week, the president of Local 909 UAW, Ghana Goodwin-Dye, had told the *Detroit Free Press*, "I believe General Motors bears the majority of the blame, but there are policies that could be put in place to hold corporations responsible for jobs in the United States, and we have to hold our politicians responsible."[3]

In the parking lot, a field of solar panels symbolized how far technology has come since the region's manufacturing heyday, back when my father was still employed by General Motors. His loyalty to the company was part of his identity, like a family name. The last forty years of changes, from automation to outsourcing to corporate bankruptcy, have left people in the region with a more measured investment in their work.

Portia Roberson, a lifelong Detroiter and the director of Focus: HOPE, a local nonprofit dedicated to ending racism, poverty, and injustice, sees the changes. "My dad, when he first came here at seventeen years of age, he was here a couple of weeks and started working at Ford Motor Company," she explains. "And then he went into the service, and he went to college on the GI Bill and all these things. But you could definitely come to Detroit or be born and raised here, and at eighteen years old, you could go work at the plant. And you could have the same house that everybody else had. You could have the two cars in the driveway. You could go on a winter and a summer vacation. You could do all the things for your family that anybody else could do."

Decades of job loss have left gaps in community and social services, but Black women have a history of being actively involved in their communities, doing a lot of work that is not accounted for in economic terms — in other words, living the core Midwestern value of lending a helping hand. This is especially apparent in programs for young people and the elderly, areas where Black women's volunteerism supports those seeking better care and more opportunity.

I witnessed this kind of dedication on a hot and gray day in mid-July, with temperatures nearing 100 degrees, as a crowd of nearly one hundred people congregated on the lawn of the McGregor Library in Highland Park for the annual Literacy in the Park Festival. This grand public library, a stately fixture on Woodward Avenue built in 1924 in a classical Roman style, has been closed since 2002, when the city went into receivership.

Under a rented white tent, more than twenty active and retired teachers listened to young people of all skill levels read out loud, for a prize of a new book and ice cream. The event was hosted by Legacy of Literacy Inc., a Highland Park nonprofit founded by retired teacher Alma Greer. The festival offers children and their families the chance to meet with authors, work on crafts, and hear music—in addition to reading, of course. The coordinated efforts of the volunteers make the experience transformative for the children. Ashelin Currie, a professor and festival organizer, greeted attendees as they made their way over to the reading tent. The vast majority of the volunteers are Black women, many of whom are also retired teachers. Their interest in creating confident young readers was evident, despite the heat. As they listened to the kids make their way through their books, it was easy to see their patience and determination being passed to the next generation.

IF DETROIT HAD NOT ALSO been the focus of so much national political attention in a few short weeks—the NAACP conference and the second Democratic national debates were also held there in July, not to mention the AfroFuture Fest, with its controversial white-people-pay-extra-admission policy—I might not have thought of these events in context with each other.[4] But I did wonder if local Black women, with their broad range of commitments, felt their experience was being represented in this political moment.

They didn't. Despite recent efforts to note Black women as a powerful political force, this essentialized perspective frequently comes without regard for geographical or economic distinctions. There is a history here. Many assume that because Black people were highly engaged by Obama's presidential campaigns, they will be eternally mobilized in support of the Democratic Party. In 2008, nearly 90 percent of eligible Black voters cast a ballot.[5] But since then, these numbers have been declining precipitously. In 2012, 66 percent of Black people voted, but by 2016, only 59 percent did.[6] This was the first time in twenty years that the Black turnout declined during a presidential election cycle.

Perhaps as a result of the #MeToo movement, or the lack of talking points directly focused on them, many Black women are finding new outlets for their energies—outside of bipartisan politics. So, while the 2020 election cycle, for many voters, looks to be a referendum on Trump, for Black women it is not yet clear if voting against a candidate will be as powerful a mobilizing force as voting for one.

According to the Census Bureau's Population Survey Voting and Registration Supplement, 70 percent of Black women exercised their right to vote in 2012, nearly 10 percent more than women of color overall.[7] Recognizing this level of participation, the Democratic National Convention vowed to engage more Black women in party leadership and strategy in 2017. In April 2019, Waikinya Clanton, who is the director of African American and women's outreach and engagement for the Democratic National Committee (DNC), executive director for the National Organization of Black Elected Legislative Women, and developer of the DNC's Seat at the Table Tour, was promoted to senior adviser for DNC chairman Tom Perez.[8]

The number of Black women serving in government is also growing. In the 2018 midterm elections, five new Black women were elected to the House of Representatives; it was an election that also saw major gains by other women of color. According to NBC News, at the International Brotherhood of Electrical Workers Local 58 on the day before the first debates in Detroit, Perez noted a need for the support of African American women.[9] "I think the African American vote here in Michigan and across the country is vital to our success," he said.

Despite being touted by progressive candidates, the 2018 Essence/BWR survey revealed an increase in the percentage of Black women who considered themselves activists.[10] There also continues to be a slight but steady decline in the party from those who identify as Democrats. This may have to do with the way the party has framed the issues. According to this poll, affordable health care is not as important to respondents as it was in 2016. (The issue of reproductive choice was singled out as a separate issue, though it was an immediate and growing concern for several women I spoke to, no matter their personal beliefs.)

A recent article by the Brookings Institution noted: "On the question of what issues are the most important, Black women cited racial inequality first at 29%, followed by health care at 21% and the growing gap between the rich and poor at 18%.[11] The economy ranked as the fourth most important issue at 11%; which, if combined with the wealth gap, would tie racial inequality as the top issue for Black women." As in 2016, turnout will be a key factor in election outcomes, and the turnout of Black women is likely to have a significant impact in Midwestern states like Michigan, which have been disproportionately impacted by policy changes in manufacturing, immigration, agriculture, and the environment. Yet these indicators do not reflect the dynamic challenges Black women in Detroit have encountered in the last decade, or how those experiences might affect their participation in the upcoming election.

• • •

**PIPER CARTER, AN ORGANIZER,** environmental justice advocate, and entrepreneur, worked on the 2012 Obama campaign, but she was not impressed with his accomplishments with regard to the Black community. Two sticking points for here were his handling of the Flint water crisis and the 2008 bank bailout—after which Detroit's economy and infrastructure faltered under the weight of its debt. "The banks had given bailouts to corporations instead of the people who had done those double mortgages under the housing crisis," Carter says. "It was a time where, in Detroit, democracy was stolen."

By 2013, Detroit had become the largest city in the United States to be taken over by a governor-appointed emergency financial manager, Kevin Orr, who assumed authority over city employees, budgets, ordinances, and city-owned property. Carter, like many other city residents, took issue with the way state officials handled the emergency management plan. "The city was forced to have a financial manager—even though the people voted against the financial manager," she says. "The financial manager decided to close the schools . . . cut off people's water . . . and put people out of their homes because of the mortgage crisis."

Distrust following Detroit's bankruptcy filing in 2013—combined with news about potential voting interference after the failure of eighty-seven voting machines in Detroit in 2016, reports of voter suppression in Georgia in 2018, and growing repercussions from the repeal of key provisions in the Voting Rights Act of 2013—have left some voters concerned about the security of their vote. According to Currie, the professor and reading festival volunteer who arrived from North Carolina for graduate study more than ten years ago and never left, "One thing is we can get out there, and then just knowing that maybe my vote really, even though I voted, my vote really didn't get counted."

While voting for the presidential candidate is important, many underestimate how Black women will weigh their decision, especially in the primaries, in a region where economic conditions have been volatile for several decades. Focus: HOPE has been responsive to these turns by providing job training, community advocacy, support for senior citizens, and antiracism work since 1968. Portia Roberson notes that along with significant job growth in hospitality and information technology, the biggest industries coming to the Detroit area are not the ones that have historically defined it. But experience has made it clear that a diverse economy is key to the stability of a city's workforce. Right now, there is a boom in the construction industry in Detroit, and with that comes new opportunities for developing skills in that area.

But that could change suddenly, too, and Roberson keeps that in the back of her mind. "I'm very sensitive to the idea that just as Focus: HOPE had been very much based in the automotive and manufacturing space in terms of workforce training," she explains, "that we don't sort of rush to construction, only to end up in a very similar situation when those jobs don't exist in a couple of years."

Detroit resident and media executive Fortman speaks of the need to hear politicians address the impact of policy on the financial well-being of Black women and their families: "In a city like Detroit, where Black women lead households more often than not, you cannot separate the term 'working-class' from Blackness, and certainly not from Black women."

She adds, "If they are ignoring that conversation, they're likely not going to motivate a large swath of the population that holds the purse strings in their household."

Author A. J. Williams, another native Detroiter, has plans to build a business and appreciates the flexibility that comes with new entrepreneurial opportunities. "We just legalized recreational cannabis," she says. "So I do want equality and inclusion at the state level, for different minorities to be able to have access to make businesses in that arena. So those are kind of my things on that level."

Likewise, Currie recognizes the impact of disparity in opportunity.

"Black women are the most educated," she says, "and we're the ones start-ing the businesses, yet we have fewer investors and less money. I don't hear any conversation around that."

Community-level concerns factor highly for those women who are socially engaged. Fortman expressed concern about the lack of serious engagement with issues that deeply affect the region: "Flint came up in both nights of the Dem debates, but it was no more than a talking point." She adds, "We are increasingly becoming a city and nation where you can get the help you need as long as you are already in the, and I say this in quotes, 'right class.' We're leaving behind—especially in a city like Detroit—children, and we're leaving behind the elderly."

Demonstrating care for others also is key to how Williams defines her values: "I grew up very Christian, and you know, I traveled a lot and I stud-ied world religion, and so my perspective is a little bit different, and it's a lot more liberal. However, on the flip side, because I grew up in a pre-dominantly African American neighborhood, I went to a predominantly African American school. I am passionate about our community like I'm passionate about African American political issues."

Carter, who worked on the national women's march in Detroit, took issue with the organization's one-size-fits-all approach to building local connections. "When they came to Detroit, we made sure that Black and Brown and Indigenous and queer and differently abled folk issues were centered. The folks in the margins' issues were centered. We decided to caucus, and we did it on our own," she explains. "It was hilarious because all the white women in the room were like, 'You guys, you can't caucus. You didn't ask permission.' I was like, 'We're not going to ask. We're talk-ing about things that impact us, and this large conglomerate of a national organization that has millions of dollars to do an event in our city is com-ing here and spending money and saying that they want to center local people and local issues, and we're holding them accountable to all of that, and that's our duty.'"

Of course, pundits proclaim that no issue compares with the importance of beating Trump. But it's clear that DNC coalition-building will need to engage a broader cohort of political perspectives than ever before to succeed in this unprecedented moment of political unrest. Those who expect a groundswell of support from Black women to carry the message may be disappointed. Failing to recognize their nuanced relationship to these issues may mean losing the Midwest, again, though this time in an entirely new way.

# THE IOWA CAUCUS: AN OBITUARY

## Courtney Crowder

T he Iowa Caucuses—the quadrennial beginning of the American presidential nominating process—are widely known as an exercise in retail politics, where an engaged body politic judges candidates' mettle in a state cheap enough that anyone, anyone, has a fair shake at snatching the crown. Alas, they went on life support on Monday evening, February 3, just after the more than 1,600 neighborhood gatherings concluded.

They were forty-eight years (or twelve cycles) old.

The caucuses' final failure, as heralded by talking heads far and wide, was a technical glitch in a delegate reporting app, a modern solution forced upon a system conspicuously rooted in colonial-era town meetings.

This telecommunications turmoil came as the perfect punctuation mark for the oft-repeated question, "Why should Iowa get to be first?" And for analysts on both sides of the aisle, the delay in reporting results, which stretched on for weeks, was yet more proof that Iowa can't handle this awesome responsibility.

"This should be the end of this nonsense with Iowa," political commentator Van Jones declared.

"This state had one job—they had one job—and they blew it!" CNN anchor Chris Cuomo proclaimed.

But as pundits prognosticated, a movement without the mouthpiece of mass media swelled throughout Iowa, reviving the moribund caucuses just as they were slipping away. Little more than twenty-four hours after the political meltdown that saw no one actually win the first-in-the-nation contest, the Iowa Caucuses endured in a sort of stasis—their long-term prognosis unclear, though they remain under close observation.

Despite the limp to the finish line in 2020, the packing of campaign offices and relocating of field organizers allowed us to call this cycle complete.

The 2020 Iowa Caucuses trace their origins to a *Washington Post* op-ed printed nearly three years ago. Within those paragraphs, former representative John Delaney announced his intention to run for the nation's highest office, hoping voters would follow him down a purple centrist path in an era—and a place—defined by vivid reds and high-definition blues.

Growing from its infancy, when candidates keynoted county soup suppers, to the mega-rallies of its nascent adulthood, the 2020 cycle quickly gained new faces and lost others. And the nation got its fill of homespun Midwest charm, through made-for-TV moments like when a college student pushed through a group gathered to hear Senator Kirsten Gillibrand and excused herself by declaring that she was "just trying to get some ranch"; former governor John Hickenlooper donning oh-so-much Spandex to ride a bicycle across the state, meeting voters and eating incredible amounts of granny pies; and California representative Eric Swalwell nudging a woman's car out of a snowbank, then directing traffic as she backed down a hill.

All along the way, Iowans braved frigid cold and sweltering heat to measure the candidates' message and moral fiber—making lists of their favorites, then ordering and reordering them (over and over).

On Caucus Day, the 2020 cycle had its first in-state test in Ottumwa, a blue-collar town saved from the dark fate of other now-boarded-up rural hamlets by an influx of immigrants working, buying property, and starting families. There, in a union hall, a group of Ethiopian pork plant workers were the first Iowans to make their selection for the Democratic nominee for president. Sporting smiles and signs, the caucus-goers gathered in the corner of the room dedicated to Senator Bernie Sanders, whose campaign had been canvassing outside JBS Pork during shift changes between midnight and 2 a.m.

Six hours before Iowans would make their choice, a group of expats in Scotland chomped on home-baked cookies and popcorn as they gathered under placards celebrating Iowa history. "Third state to declare same-sex marriage constitutional," read one. "No other state had a higher percentage of men serve the Union in the Civil War," declared another.

Started by six friends, more than a dozen fellow Iowans joined this "satellite" caucus, including a woman who flew in from Germany and a man who traveled from Italy. They may have been strangers when the caucus began, but they left as friends, bonded by Iowa roots even as they live thousands of miles from the Hawkeye State.

Just before lunch, a group of fourth and fifth graders from Des Moines gathered to learn about the caucus process. A show of hands revealed that most of the kids planned to attend the caucus that evening with their parents. One curious girl raised her hand and asked if Senator Elizabeth Warren was going to become the "first girl" president that night.

Not that night, I said, but maybe in November. She looked at me, tilted her head so her ponytail swished to the other side, and said, "I really hope that happens."

In a YMCA gym, Latin music greeted hundreds of Latinx Iowans filing in for a bilingual caucus. "The more people come out today, that vote and participate, the better things will be for us," said Ana Correa, eighteen, a first-time voter.

In a different bilingual caucus, where Sanders dominated, a Warren supporter used the time normally set aside for him to persuade caucusgoers to his candidate's side to, instead, thank his Latinx community for participating "in large numbers."

In the lobby of a downtown Hilton, Iowan Chris Taylor and his cousin Amy Tish, of Maryland, took a break from their tour of his home state. Putting a few hundred miles on their rental car, the pair saw seven candidates—changing flights and driving from Chicago when a layover threatened their plans—laughing, debating, eating breakfast pizza, and growing closer than they had ever been.

Removing their shoes as they entered the worship space at the Bosnian Islamic Center mosque, caucus-goers discovered a diverse precinct where some neighbors hailed from Bosnia or Bhutan, while others were of Mexican or Asian descent. After voters identified a language barrier, one of the gathered Iowans, Deven Sapkota, volunteered to translate the caucus chair's speech into Nepali. He wanted to make sure everyone understood the process and knew exactly for whom they were voting.

At an early caucus site sponsored by the Central Iowa Center for Independent Living, Carol Schroeder, sixty-five, of Des Moines, reveled in a site that was truly accessible to people with disabilities. As someone who uses a walker, she worries over what accommodations caucus sites might have—or not have. But with free pizza, plentiful water, gender-neutral bathrooms, a lactation room, a quiet room, and a kids' area, the organizers had thought of everything, she told me.

Party leadership was "finally listening" to what disabled people had been requesting for years, she said. At that same caucus was Aidan Zingler, thirty-five, of Des Moines, who has panic attacks in large crowds. They—Zingler's preferred pronoun—had never managed to make it to the end of a caucus, but, after a brief trip to the quiet room, their vote was counted for the first time.

At one of the largest caucus gatherings in Des Moines, Scott Matter, a precinct chair for former mayor Pete Buttigieg, almost cried after his crew gave Pete a win. A lifelong Republican who worked for heavyweights like Senators Chuck Grassley and Bob Dole, Matter tells me he changed his registration after the GOP abandoned ideals he thought were central to the party's foundation. Now, as a first-time Democrat, he got to make sure those principles were preserved.

In that same precinct, almost 300 people registered to vote. At an Iowa City gathering, 100 people registered. The Dallas County Democrats, a mostly suburban group, registered 2,000 new voters. And in rural northwest Iowa, where blowing wind turned the thermostat down to 18 degrees, almost a third of their caucus-goers were new—and young—voters.

And in a nondescript room in a mostly empty strip mall, a historic first amid a night of firsts almost went unnoticed. There, out of sight from the big broadcast news cameras, eighteen Iowans discussed, debated, and caucused for presidential nominees in their own language at the American Sign Language caucus. The group's leaders believe this marked the first ASL presidential caucus ever on American shores.

Never has silence spoken so loudly.

Across the state, people gave up their time and their energy to abandon echo chambers and discuss topics and pick nominees in public. They didn't passively engage—just writing a check or signing a petition or snarking on Facebook—they spoke with their feet and their hearts.

Run by almost entirely all volunteers, the caucuses really are politics at the lowest common denominator.

They are a moment when policies are drafted by the people, for the people, and of the people. They are a time when individuals can be included in the bedrock of our American culture; a time when their choices can be seen and their voices heard. They are a process meant to form a powerfully connected community, not to satisfy the insatiable need to bet on the next horse race.

And in this globalized, digital world, they seem a reminder that despite all the ways our society could fracture, there really is more uniting us than dividing us.

So as pundits declare the 2020 Iowa Caucuses the last of the first, these are the moments that will be indelible in my mind. Remember, in the Midwest, we survive the long winter, and somewhere deep in my soul, I don't think this is good-bye.

Recall: "This state had one job," Chris Cuomo said as an empty results graphic splayed across CNN screens. "And they blew it!"

He's only half right. We did have one job: for the citizens who left each gym, church, auditorium, and local hall to be more engaged and more connected than they were when they went in.

Whatever the election results, that job got done on Caucus Night 2020.

# IN PRAISE OF THE ROOKIE

## Heather Sinclair Shaw

When I knock on the door of the old Hebron United Methodist Church, I am greeted by Medusa, a giant fawn mastiff squirming enthusiastically in the foyer. Her owner, Valerie Mockus, ushers me to a dining table that sits where the altar once stood. A large kitchen is laid out behind it; below, the former sanctuary is a spacious living room filled with light from the wide lancet windows that line both walls. I am struck by how the space effortlessly holds two identities; it is at once church and house, and seems, like Valerie herself, unruffled by this. Outside a sign reads simply: "The Chouse, a private residence."

Valerie is my accountability partner. We met at a networking event up the road in Newark, Ohio, and found we had much in common as women in midlife, juggling our responsibilities to work, home, and community. We meet regularly to help each other; we drink tea and talk about goal setting while Medusa pushes the small boulder of her nose into my shoe.

Valerie was born in the small village of Hebron, Ohio, which sits where the Ohio & Erie Canal intersected with the old National Road on

35

its meandering path from Lake Erie down to the Ohio River. The village center is now Canal Park, a small green space that sits on the old tow path. Valerie went to Sunday school in the church she now calls home. Her mother was married here. Her great-great-grandparents were stewards. So when Valerie and her husband, Gary, decided to move back to Hebron from Florida in 2015 and found that the church was up for auction, they went for it. Gary wanted a building that was "architecturally interesting," she jokes.

Not long after they finally relocated in 2017, Mike McFarland, then mayor of Hebron, stopped by for a visit—perhaps, at first, just to see what was up with the couple who had bought a church. But Valerie found Mike supportive and kind, and soon they were brainstorming ways to create a more vibrant community in Hebron. Eventually the mayor approached Valerie with an idea: What about a food festival? There's the Paw Paw Festival in Albany, the Pumpkin Festival in Circleville, the Swiss Festival in Sugarcreek. Valerie suggested a potato festival. "You can do *anything* with a potato!" she recalls.

"I was thinking of a pie festival," Mike told her. Valerie owns a tech consulting firm called Apple Pi. She laughs, remembering the moment. That's a much better idea, she said.

Valerie agreed to chair the committee, though she had never managed a festival; she'd never even volunteered at one. But she loved her village and wanted to see it grow and thrive. That same spring, Mike approached Valerie with another, bigger idea. He'd been serving the village of Hebron for a long time, first as an administrator, then as the mayor. He was ready to retire, and he was looking for a replacement. If Valerie was willing to run, Mike said, he would endorse her.

**VALERIE WAS RETICENT AT FIRST.** She likes to be prepared, and this was something she couldn't possibly be prepared for. But she remembers the moment she decided to go for it. Her book club had been reading Sheryl Sandberg's *Lean In*; halfway down a right-facing page, she had an epiphany. *I'm worried that I'm not 100 percent qualified, but there's someone out there who's only 60 percent qualified and has already applied.* "And I thought, you know what? I run my own business, I have a doctorate, I care about this community, I'm invested. I don't have any mayoral experience, but most people who run for local office don't."

Valerie also recognized that she was in a privileged position. Her work allowed her the flexibility to make her own schedule, and be home when she needed to be. There are obstacles to running for any political position: most people don't have jobs that allow them to serve, or they can't afford to campaign. The signage alone is expensive.

Not to mention the current political environment. Public trust in government remains at an all-time low, which Valerie felt keenly while circulating her mayoral petition in Hebron. It can be a real barrier for folks at the local level, who want to make a difference in their communities but are concerned about taking on the stigma that sometimes comes with public office. But Valerie agreed, and by late spring she was planning in earnest for the Hebron Pie Festival and circulating her petition at the same time.

They baked 265 pies in four days. Volunteers donned hair nets, peeled apples, rolled out hundreds of homemade crusts. They filled convection ovens over and over again. Valerie's hands unconsciously mime the crank of an apple corer as she remembers the scene.

Her mayoral petition was due the following week, but Valerie was slated to be away for a professional training. So on the last day of baking, dusted in flour and smelling of apples, Valerie walked into the Licking County Board of Elections to turn in her petition signatures.

The woman behind the desk looked at the paperwork and then at Valerie. "Are you sure you want to turn this in?" she asked.

"Yes, I'm sure. What are you talking about?" Valerie said. She was testy and tired. She'd been baking pies and painting signs for the festival all day.

"Are you sure you want to turn this in?" the woman behind the desk asked again.

Looking back on it now, Valerie admits that anyone who'd ever been in politics would've taken this as a sign. But Valerie was not a politician.

"Yes, I want to turn it in. Why do I feel like I'm being hazed right now?" she said a little too loudly.

Another person in the office walked up, took her paperwork, certified it, and told Valerie that she could leave.

"What about this other form?" she asked.

"You won't be needing that."

THAT SATURDAY, about two thousand people turned out for the first annual Hebron Pie Festival. A giant red and white tent was erected in the small green space at the intersection of Main and High Streets. There was a bake-off, a pie-eating contest, live music, and, of course, a pie-*throwing* contest. They ran out of pies in the first few hours; volunteers ran to GFS and Kroger for ready-made and frozen pies to bring back and bake. "It was a rookie mistake," Valerie says. "We learned a lot of things the hard way that first year."

On August 9, the local newspaper, the *Newark Advocate*, ran an article about Valerie's mayoral run. It turns out she was the lone candidate. She was endorsed by McFarland. As long as her petition signatures were approved and there was no write-in, her run would be uncontested. It seemed inevitable.

But Valerie's petition signatures were not approved.

Right after the article ran, Valerie got a phone call from Luke Burton, director of the Licking County Board of Elections. "This is the worst part of my job," he began.

While she was out collecting signatures, Valerie visited an elderly woman I'll call Jean in her home. When Jean found out Valerie was running for mayor she said, "I don't think women should be in office."

Valerie didn't skip a beat. "I get that," she said. "I'm pretty sure that if my grandmother was alive, she would've said the same thing to someone like me." But instead of walking away, Valerie stayed. She asked questions and listened to the answers. She understood that whatever Jean's political views were, her voice was just as relevant as every other Hebron resident.

As Valerie prepared to leave, Jean said, "Do you have your petition with you?"

"It's okay," Valerie said. "I respect your opinion."

"Well, just because I wouldn't vote for a woman doesn't mean you shouldn't be on the ballot!" Jean said.

Valerie's face brightens as she tells me the story later. "That, to me, was a great interaction. I don't know if she would've voted for me or not. It really doesn't matter. If I moved her needle at all, it was worth it."

Valerie earned dozens of signatures one by one by talking with residents like Jean and listening to their concerns. Because she was concerned about appearing trustworthy, and wanted to make sure all of her signatures were approved, Valerie only allowed one other person to circulate the petition on her behalf: Mayor McFarland.

The signatures McFarland collected were accepted; Valerie's were not. Because she circulated the petition herself, she was required to file as both candidate and circulator. She filled out the "candidate" portion of the petition and left the "circulator" section blank, since the information was the same. It was a clerical error, a rookie mistake. The woman who accepted Valerie's petition would've seen it immediately, but Ohio law prohibits boards of elections officials from prechecking petitions before they are filed. Ostensibly the goal is to prevent bias. But in 2019, there were ten potential candidates disqualified from running for local office in Licking County. All, including Valerie, were running for nonpartisan positions.

All of Valerie's work was nullified in a single moment; she wasn't even permitted to run as a write-in. In November, Hebron had two write-in candidates, and zero names on the ballot for mayor.

The frustration is still there, in Valerie's shoulders, as she tells me the story months later. "It was me. It was just me. I didn't know I had to fill out both sides," she says helplessly. "I already had my signs. I have one thousand bumper stickers, if you'd like one." I can't even force a smile. I want to take them all. As her accountability partner, I've come to rely on Valerie's optimism, her intelligence, her thoroughness. I've seen firsthand how committed she is to her vision, how much she loves her home and her work. It's like something out of a Kafka novel: the one person in a small village who wants to step up and lead is prevented from doing so by a detail so bureaucratic and trivial it seems unfit for fiction. But that's exactly what happened.

"It's something that seems very arbitrary, and I hate that we can't help people," Luke Burton told the *Columbus Dispatch* in November, calling the petition process antiquated. "I don't think there should be barriers."

**JAMES LAYTON,** a longtime member of Hebron Village Council, ran as a write-in candidate for mayor and won the November election. But Valerie's optimism was resilient. In January she was appointed to village council, to the vacant seat left by Layton when he became mayor. Her desire to help her community is still palpable. Just like the Chouse, which effortlessly honors the old while welcoming the new, Valerie wants to bring a new sense of purpose to the village she loves.

"I just read a 380-page book on Robert's Rules of Order so I can follow the rules," she confesses with a smile. "I want to do a good job." This is the Valerie I know. She talks about her travels, about the hundreds of little villages she's seen across America, how she wants to learn from the successful ones and bring that back to her village. "When I see towns that are thriving, I think, We could totally be doing this."

She's the first council member to have a public Facebook page, though she was urged to take it down when she got her first threatening private message. But Valerie was undeterred. "This guy's voice is important, too," she said. "And Facebook is where people are. We have to meet them where they are."

For now that page is still live, and Valerie has already groomed the new committee chair for the second annual Hebron Pie Festival. Will she run for mayor again? She's not certain. But she knows this at least: next year, they will make more pies.

# Constituent
# Concerns

# COMPROMISED

## A Group of Small-Town Environmentalists Wanted to Stop a Potentially Toxic Costco Chicken Plant. How Did They End Up Fighting Alongside Anti-Muslim Xenophobes?

### Ted Genoways

The fire hall in Nickerson, Nebraska, population 350, was packed. The metal chairs set up for the planning board meeting were all taken. There was no room left in the aisles. Folks had squeezed into the back of the room, and the crowd stretched out the front doors and into the parking lot, where the latecomers were left pacing in the gathering dark. Most Monday nights, the village board is lucky if one or two people show up to voice an opinion on municipal matters. But on April 4, 2016, there were hundreds—so many that the board moved the meeting to a larger room and opened the windows so the people outside could hear.

The zoning committee was planning to act on a proposal that had caught the attention of everyone in the area. An unnamed company wanted to build a massive chicken-processing plant, designated in filings only as "Project Rawhide," on a tract of agricultural land about halfway to Fremont, a larger town a few miles to the south. The plant, according to a report submitted by the company, would create 1,100 new meatpacking jobs, support 125 area farmers by buying 1.6 million chickens per week, and bring in an estimated 2,000 additional jobs indirectly linked to the project. As people poured into the fire hall, someone from the Greater Fremont Development Council, which had courted the project, handed out fact sheets claiming that it would bring in a quarter of a billion dollars in revenue.

Randy Ruppert didn't buy the math. He farmed 220 acres not far from the planned site just outside Fremont, where he had retired after forty-eight years of working for railroad companies as a manager of major construction projects. He was trained to think through problems systematically, and he envisioned a host of undiscussed downsides: truck traffic, odor, inadequate waste disposal, public health risks. One of his last assignments at RailWorks Track Systems had been to help the meatpacking giant Cargill head off the swamping of its corn-milling plant in Blair, Nebraska, about twenty miles east of Nickerson, during the Missouri River flood of 2011. The city of Blair had raced to stack a mile of sandbags around its municipal wastewater-treatment facility, and Cargill ended up building an eight-foot-high, three-mile-long emergency levee at a cost of more than $20 million. This new poultry plant was to be sited squarely in the floodplain of the Lower Platte River. What would happen when heavy rains came again?

The Lower Platte's watershed was already classified as the sixth most polluted in the United States, thanks to another Cargill plant, in Schuyler, Nebraska, thirty miles upstream. Ruppert had become something of an environmentalist in his retirement, trying to persuade area corn and

46

soybean growers to switch to no-till farming and to plant buffer strips along their streams to keep their fertilizers from adding to the toxic runoff. He even restored sixty-five acres of his own pastureland to high-diversity prairie. Millions of chickens would not only undo that work but also leave the river water unsuitable—even untreatable—for drinking. Discreetly, he began talking to neighbors. Ruppert is an unassuming man, gregarious but soft-spoken, a blue-jeans-and-ball-cap guy who earns respect with his precise attention to detail. (He likes to relax by engraving decorative designs into rifle parts under a microscope.) After he'd spent a few days laying out his concerns, hand-painted signs started appearing along the highway: NO PROJECT RAWHIDE, CHICKENS STINK, COMING SOON: BIRD FLU.

Ruppert also decided to contact Jane Kleeb, the founder of a nonprofit advocacy group called Bold Nebraska, which had become the leading force in the state against the proposed Keystone XL pipeline. For nearly eight years, Kleeb had kept that project on hold by rallying farmers and ranchers around concerns over contamination of surface and groundwater in the event of a spill—until finally, in November 2015, President Barack Obama announced that he was rejecting the plan. (President Trump has reversed that decision, but Bold Nebraska's efforts continue to hold up construction in Nebraska.) Ruppert figured Kleeb could help him build opposition to what he considered another threat to the state's waterways by contacting the people on Bold Nebraska's mailing list and its followers on social media. Ruppert spoke with Kleeb on the phone a couple of times, and she agreed to come to the board meeting in Nickerson and even go to his home beforehand to talk with people from the community about how to fight the plant.

Kleeb told me that she wanted to get a feel for the commitment of Ruppert's group "to see if there was a winnable campaign," but she also wanted a clear sense of everyone's motives. Fremont is an old meatpacking town that has been transformed in recent decades by the industry's use of undocumented labor. In that time, the community has also become synonymous with America's rising nativist sentiment, due to a protracted and bitter legal battle it waged against undocumented Hispanic workers at the Hormel Foods plant in town. When Bold Nebraska alerted its membership online to local concerns about Project Rawhide, several of them raised objections to being seen as partnering with xenophobes and racists.

Kleeb decided to go to Fremont anyway. At Ruppert's home, she warned everyone about the perception problem, and said they needed to limit their protests to concerns about water quality. Afterward, on the drive to the fire hall, her minivan fell in with a caravan of pickups and SUVs. "I was following this guy who had a Tea Party bumper sticker and a pro-gun bumper sticker," she said. The driver was Doug Wittmann, the head of Win It Back, the local Tea Party organization. (He also happened to be Randy Ruppert's brother-in-law.) After they parked along Nickerson's main drag, Wittmann approached Kleeb on the sidewalk and asked her what she thought of his stickers. If Kleeb's years of organizing fiercely conservative ranchers in the Nebraska Sandhills had taught her anything, it was to build alliances around issues rather than identity. "Here's the thing," she told Wittmann. "We're definitely not going to agree on gun policy, but we will agree on water and property rights."

The crowd inside the fire hall was unexpectedly tense. The zoning committee had announced that it would take no comments from the community; the members just wanted to rule on the procedural question of reclassifying the property to commercial use. If anyone wanted to take up larger issues, they should talk to the village board, which would meet immediately afterward. With that, the committee voted unanimously to approve the rezoning. A ripple of anger coursed through the room. Some people got up to leave, thinking that the project was already a done deal.

When everyone was herded back into the meeting room after the break, the village board asked if anyone wanted to speak. John Wiegert, a local schoolteacher who had driven up to the meeting from Fremont with his sister, said that he'd intended to sit quietly. But after an awkward pause, and with no one rising to take the floor, he stood up.

"Hell, I'll talk," Wiegert said.

The development council had been handing out fliers touting the new jobs this project was going to create, he said, but how was a town this size going to fill three thousand new positions? "I'm worried about the type of workers that this will attract," he said. He knew that in recent years the meatpacking industry had turned away from undocumented Hispanic labor. New workers now typically had legal status, but that didn't mean they were U.S. citizens. In the poultry industry, many of the workers were political refugees from Somalia. "Being a Christian, I don't want Somalis in here," he said. "They're of Muslim descent."

Ruppert says that he shook his head, quietly cursing Wiegert's every word. This was exactly what Kleeb and Bold Nebraska had told them not to do. But Wiegert pressed on. "You know where they're going to live?" he asked. "In our neighborhoods." He pointed, one by one, to people around the room. "They're going to live next to you and you and you—and me."

At the end of the night, the board unanimously rejected the proposed plant.


**AFTER COSTCO ANNOUNCED** the move to Fremont, Randy Ruppert decided it was time to get organized. He had already taken to calling his loose-knit group of anti-Costco protesters Nebraska Communities United, but there was little more to it than a website where he shared information. To defeat Costco, he needed a formal structure, elected leaders, a real plan. Ruppert again called Jane Kleeb and asked if she could help him turn his ragtag group of family, friends, and neighbors into a durable opposition. Kleeb not only agreed, she went one better: she contacted Dave Domina, an Omaha attorney with a reputation as something of a white knight for small farmers in Nebraska. Domina has represented the landowners suing TransCanada over Keystone XL, corn growers suing the seed giant Syngenta after China rejected their GMO crop, and farmers suing Monsanto claiming that its herbicide RoundUp was damaging their organic crops. Domina even ran for U.S. Senate against Fremont native Ben Sasse in 2014—though in heavily Republican Nebraska, he was defeated in a landslide.

Ruppert hoped that the group would heed Domina's advice and focus on environmental concerns. "This is not about nationalism," he said. "This is not about closed-mindedness." Ruppert told me that the real concern was whether Fremont's wastewater treatment facility was equipped to handle the demands of such a large poultry processor. Costco had already acknowledged that wastewater from the plant would contain fat, blood, ingesta, and fecal matter, as well as processing chemicals such as ammonia hydroxide, chlorine, and peracetic acid. The company promised that all solids and fats would be removed within the plant; the remaining waste would go to a complex of covered anaerobic lagoons, which the city agreed to finance and place under the supervision of the Nebraska Department of Environmental Quality.

But Ruppert pointed out that the whole system would use about two million gallons of water per day, and the lagoons were estimated to occupy a stunning forty acres. If the Lower Platte ever flooded, as the Missouri did just a few years ago, these lagoons could release a deluge of toxic chemicals. Even normal runoff from hundreds of new chicken barns would threaten to carry nitrates and phosphorous into the river from the "litter" of the 150 million birds that Costco hoped to slaughter each year. This volume of waste created a larger, and very specific, public health concern. The Lower Platte is one of the primary sources of drinking water for Omaha and Lincoln, cities with a combined population of nearly a million people.

Consider, then, the bind in which people in Fremont like Ruppert find themselves. While he disliked the prospect of being called a racist for allying his movement with an avowed Islamophobe like Wiegert, he worried that simply shunning Wiegert and the many townspeople who agreed with him would split the opposition to Costco—and ultimately speed the construction of a plant that would profit from immigrant labor and pose a direct threat to the health of people of color. "If you want to talk about being a racist," Ruppert said, "this corporate model of farming is pure racism." So, instead, he decided to see if he could convince his neighbors to stick to environmental grounds and leave immigration out of it.

The meeting Ruppert called with Domina was held at the home of Debby Durham, a friend who lived on the north side of Fremont. Durham had risen at the most recent Fremont city council meeting to express her opposition to Costco over concerns about avian flu—but also the worry she shared with John Wiegert. "Our town is in jeopardy, not only with disease," she said, "but illegals. Eleven hundred of them." Durham had invited Wiegert to the meeting, which Ruppert decided, after some debate, was a good idea. He didn't share Wiegert and Durham's views on immigration, but he had to admit that they were passionate opponents of the plant. If he could convince them to focus on the public safety concerns, then he thought they deserved a place in the group.

Once everyone was seated in the living room of Durham's sprawling farmhouse, Domina rose to speak. If the group wanted to stop the chicken plant, he said, they had to focus on water quality, unfair contracts, and the abuses of public domain that almost always attend such projects. "Don't talk about immigration; don't talk about the workers," he said, according to several people who attended the meeting. (Domina did not respond to repeated requests to comment for this story.) Wiegert told me that he assumed Domina's remarks were made directly to him, but he says he remained silent. "Wasn't my meeting." To break the tension, Doug Wittmann, Ruppert's brother-in-law, jumped in. "Look," he said, pointing at

Kleeb, "we have wacky liberals. We have wacky conservatives," gesturing toward Wiegert, "and we have some libertarians. But we can all fight this social disgrace."

**COSTCO'S APPLICATION** to build the plant kept sailing through the Fremont city council's approval process. The new site, on farmland just outside the city limits, was annexed into the town, then rezoned from agricultural to commercial, and then declared blighted and substandard, all maneuvers that allowed the town to offer Costco more than $13 million in tax incentives. When objections were raised over condemning productive farmland, the size of the allotted area was stretched to include some abandoned buildings close by. Through it all, people from Fremont gathered, in person and online, in attempts to unify over their opposition to the plant. But deep rifts were soon exposed.

Jerry Hart, one of John Wiegert's co-petitioners on the anti-immigration ordinance, was a regular, and confrontational, presence on a Facebook group called Fremont City Council Watchdog. One local resident mocked him, writing, "yes, you should be so 'proud' of your illegal ordinance, that accomplishes nothing, and made Fremont a laughingstock. . . . And so many of those you think are illegal are not. They have as much a right to be here as you do. You, sir, are un-American." Hart replied, "Illegal is not a race. Mexican is not a race. Muslim is not a race. You are stupid and you can't fix stupid."

After similar statements at small-group community meetings hosted by the Greater Fremont Development Council, Walt Shafer from Lincoln Premium Poultry, a Costco subcontractor that would manage the plant, announced that no one from his company or Costco would attend a larger, city-wide gathering scheduled to be held at a meeting hall south of the railroad tracks. "We're not going to meet with a lynch mob," Shafer said. After another meeting hosted by Nebraska Communities United in

September, I was approached by a man named Gene Schultz, a member of Doug Wittmann's Tea Party group, who told me that he had changed his position somewhat on Mexican workers at Hormel. "At least they're not Muslims," he said. "Muslims will cut your head off." Later, I looked up his lengthy Change.org signing statement, which included a warning that if Costco were allowed to build its plant, the Muslim call to prayer would blare from loudspeakers in Fremont five times per day. "When hundreds of Somali or Syrian Muslims come to our town they will change our culture," he wrote. "These are typically uneducated, sharia-loving Muslims that have no concept of our Constitution, laws, or modern way of life."

Wiegert, meanwhile, was a regular presence at the city council meetings, loudly railing against Costco's putative workforce. He was also a reliable source for inflammatory statements in the media. When reporters called, he always denied being a racist and instead talked about legal immigration and the rule of law, the impact that refugee children would have on local schools, and his belief that communities should be able to decide "who they do or do not want as neighbors." Inevitably, though, he would veer off course, and insist that there is good reason to be afraid of Muslims, and Somalis in particular, given instances of terrorism around the world. He told one reporter he didn't want a single Somali in his town: "Even if there's one, there's one too many." He talked to the *Omaha World-Herald*, the state's largest newspaper; went on American Public Media's *Marketplace*; and even gave Katie Couric a guided tour of Fremont for a documentary series set to air next year on the National Geographic channel, driving her around the trailer park south of town where most of the "illegals" live.

Ruppert did everything he could to counter Wiegert. "Animosity needs to be set aside," he told the local newspaper. "We need to proceed with the facts as we know them, and proceed in a way that does not divide the community." And his environmental message did seem to have an impact—to an extent. In December, after repeated demonstrations that the land in question was in a floodplain—and barely a half mile from the main channel of the Platte River—the city council approved tax-increment financing to assist with relocating the covered lagoons from the Costco site to land adjoining the wastewater-treatment facility, three miles away. But this short-term victory proved costly. With no council debate, the private farmland was earmarked for acquisition by the city via eminent domain—and with the improved sewage treatment, Costco then applied to expand the size of the plant onto additional land, increasing production to more than two million chickens per week. The new plan was unanimously approved by the city council. What's more, after Donald Trump was elected president, the fear of the Department of Housing and Urban Development (HUD) suing Fremont over its anti-immigration ordinance also eased; the city raided the $2 million legal defense fund and used the money to address infrastructure needs expressed by Costco.

Ruppert knew he needed help from large environmental groups to keep up. He couldn't research the new site, look into the new sewage plan, and investigate the companies slated to complete the work; it was too much to do alone. He turned to national environmental organizations for assistance, but they were of little use. "I'm incredibly disappointed in the Big Greens," Ruppert told me. "I don't know what they do with their money. I truly don't. We've had little to no help—a lot of 'support'—but where are you on these issues? These are the issues that you're supposed to be fighting for." Without assistance from the outside, Ruppert and Nebraska Communities United reluctantly decided to shift their message away from opposing Costco on environmental grounds and toward fighting the city of Fremont on its use of eminent domain.

Doug Wittmann, for one, was delighted by the change. As a Tea Party true believer, he strongly opposed the idea of government being able to take away private land for any reason. "The right to life, liberty, and the pursuit of happiness—or property—being among the rights that God gives us, is sacred," he told me. Wittmann was able to rally renewed support from his group, and Dave Domina, who had extensive experience in eminent domain law from working with landowners on the Keystone XL route, said he was willing to help with a legal challenge to this use of governmental power for private corporations. He agreed to draw up the language for a ballot measure to officially curb the eminent domain powers of the city of Fremont.

To get Domina's measure onto the ballot, the Costco opponents had to get enough people to sign a petition supporting it. And who among them had more experience in putting together walking lists and working with canvassers? Who had shown more tenacity in making calls and going door-to-door collecting signatures? It took some doing, but finally Ruppert agreed to Wittmann's suggestion for the named lead petitioner: John Wiegert.

**I ASKED JANE KLEEB,** who in June 2016 became chair of the Nebraska Democratic Party, if she thought that eminent domain was being used in Fremont as a fig leaf to place over another xenophobic campaign. She rejected that idea outright. She conceded that Wiegert had "warped views on immigrants" but bristled at the implication that working with him tainted her own efforts. "The only way that we're going to win these big political fights is with unlikely alliances," she said. "This was true on the pipeline, too. A lot of the farmers and ranchers have different political views on other issues, but we were all on the same page for stopping Keystone XL." Kleeb also said she believed that these "unlikely" partnerships can unstick the political gridlock in a deep red state like Nebraska — and perhaps even in America. "The more you work alongside each other, shoulder to shoulder, the more difficult it becomes to demonize each other," she said. "That's the biggest thing: You will start to change people's minds — and your mind will start to change on certain things — even while we still disagree on some fundamental issues."

It's a noble sentiment, but I couldn't ignore the darker forces that seemed to be driving at least part of Fremont's opposition to the Costco plant. Earlier that year, I had reported on another heartland town roiled by an influx of Muslim workers at a meatpacking plant. According to the FBI, white supremacists had planned a large-scale bomb attack on the homes of a community of Somali refugees in Garden City, Kansas. If Fremont's often vulgar opinions about Muslim outsiders, conflating them with terrorists, blossomed into violence, what responsibility would everyone involved bear for not loudly denouncing the xenophobic and Islamophobic rhetoric from the very beginning? Kleeb and Ruppert, and perhaps even Dave Domina, may hold out hopes of softening the hearts of their strange political bedfellows, but when I asked Wiegert, at his home one night, if he had "evolved" by working with Nebraska Communities United, Bold Nebraska, and now the state Democratic Party, he dismissed the idea. He wasn't interested in being converted to anyone else's cause, and he didn't expect to win converts to his.

"I'm not against Muslims," Wiegert repeated. "It's not like I hate them, but I will say: It's a worry." He glanced up at the TV. He had the sound off, but the Fox News talking heads still pantomimed their anger, while the crawl at the bottom of the screen demanded an investigation of Hillary Clinton's Russian ties. "They come from rogue nations. And they don't get how we live. So it can upset a city, upset a state. It scares me. It really does."

Before Wiegert could get his petition campaign under way, the city executed yet another legal end run. To avoid an eminent domain fight, they made a preemptive bid on the farmland neighboring the wastewater-treatment facility—reportedly offering the owners nearly three times what surrounding property typically sells for. Ruppert told me he had already talked to Domina and to Kleeb, and they were looking into guidelines governing how much a municipality can legally spend to obtain a property for a project. So the fight continues, but the more fundamental questions have yet to be reckoned with: Are environmentalists succeeding in winning the nativists over to their way of thinking? Or have they been co-opted into the xenophobic cause?

Wiegert, for his part, said he still couldn't understand why anyone in Fremont would be more concerned about Omaha's water than a Muslim moving in next door. "Heck," he said, "you've got a president saying, 'Let's put a ban on these people until we can get something to make sure that these people coming in are coming for the right reason.'" He pointed at me, for emphasis, as if the cameras were watching. "The American dream."

# BODIES ON THE LINE

## Protest, Politics, and Power
## on an Appalachian Railroad

### Sydney Boles

lackjewel LLC ran coal mines in Kentucky, Virginia, West Virginia, and Wyoming. On July 1, 2019, it declared bankruptcy, leaving some 1,700 people jobless.

Three days before this, on June 28, workers received paychecks that went toward rent, mortgage, utilities, birthday presents, food, and other typical expenses. Those checks bounced, leaving many in the hole with their banks. The checks they should have received in mid-July—their final ones—never came. The employees were told not to come to work, but they weren't officially laid off, and because they weren't officially laid off, they struggled to access unemployment benefits. Miners couldn't reach anyone at Blackjewel. For weeks, no one had a clue what was going on.

On Monday, July 29, after weeks of confusion during which families had already been dipping into nest eggs to make ends meet, a woman who lived near the railroad tracks in Harlan County, Kentucky, saw a train being loaded up with coal at a Blackjewel loading plant. She sent a text around to people she knew who worked at the mine. Hang on, she asked. Isn't Blackjewel supposed to be bankrupt? How are they moving this coal?

A miner named Chris Sexton received that text and rallied some of his buddies. Sexton and four other men drove to Gilley's Hollow Road, where they scrambled up onto the tracks in front of the idling train.

"If they can move this train, they can give us our money!" miner Shane Smith told me.

That first afternoon, the local cops politely asked the miners to get off the coal company's property, so they moved about a half a mile down the road to a strip of land beside Highway 119. A couple of the miners' wives showed up, one with a case of water and another, Felicia Cress, with a cardboard pizza box on which she had written "NO PAY WE STAY" in permanent marker. "This happened because we got shafted, which happens all the time," Cress told me. "You got these rich people that shit on these poor people, and people just overlook it."

With a silver pickup parked across the tracks and a camping chair teetering on the crossties, to a sound track of tinny country music from the phones of anyone whose battery hadn't yet died, the small crew partied through the night, drunk on "big boy juice" and the thrill of direct action. It felt like anything could happen. Would the cops come back? Would there be a fight? How seriously were these guys taking this?

That night, the men resolved not to move until they got their pay.

They blocked that train for fifty-nine days.

It was ragtag and chaotic for a few days, but soon enough, a full-on camp sprouted. Miners pitched a canopy tent over the railroad. Beside the tracks, miners' wives and girlfriends set up a functioning kitchen, where ample donations from local supporters were alchemized into warm meals. Families brought their kids, who played touch football and cornhole near the tracks.

There was firebrand Felicia Cress and her quiet husband, Curtis, who had never wanted to be a miner in the first place. Chris and Stacy Rowe assumed the role of spokespeople. David Pratt Jr. was frequently at the camp with his wife, Wendy, and their young children. David's father, David Sr., was just one year away from retirement when the bankruptcy hit, and he was worried he might have cancer. There was James Belt, a middle-aged man who came on his own and really just wanted his money. And there was Bobby Sexton, who was so scared about providing for his family.

I was there for as much of it as I could be. I was working at WMMT, a community radio station just over the mountain from Harlan County, and writing radio and Web stories for a network of NPR member stations in Kentucky, Ohio, and West Virginia. I was there early in the morning, when miners and their wives poked bleary heads out of their tents, and in the heat of those August afternoons when things slowed down enough for more thoughtful conversations. I held miners' babies; I nodded and listened while men cycled through anger and grief and hopelessness, not only because they hadn't been paid, but because their very ability to feed their children was dependent on an industry that was dying.

All the while, $1.4 million worth of coal idled up the tracks, heat waves rising from it in the summer sun. Miners told me that if the blockade went on much longer, and the heat didn't let up, the internal temperature of the blockaded coal could cause the whole train to catch fire.

Journalists from Washington, D.C., and New York City flocked to the scene. They spent a few hours pretending to feel at ease, trying to make their questions seem casual, and the core of regular protesters repeated their stories until they felt like talking points.

One reason the story was so irresistible was the history of the place: It was the county once known as "Bloody Harlan," after a series of labor clashes between miners and coal company owners in the 1930s. Central Appalachia has long been defined in popular understanding by one industry, and lately, one particular Republican president. Phrases like "the heart of coal country" and "Trump Country" were always present, even if they went unspoken.

When the journalists' stories appeared online, Felicia and Stacy pored over each one, searching for hints of the hillbilly stereotypes they were committed to rebutting. They almost always found some. Appalachian people are stereotyped as lazy, stupid, and behind the times, and coal miners are a particular target. Liberals paternalize them, as evidenced by comments on my Twitter feed: that those hillbillies had voted against their own interests and deserved their suffering. Even Karl Marx likely would have dismissed them as part of the "lumpenproletariat"—a lower stratum of society devoid of class consciousness, unradicalizable, reacting only to their immediate circumstances.

But those mischaracterizations strip Appalachia of its complexity. "Bloody Harlan" was the site of violent union organizing against the coal companies in the 1920s and again in the 1970s. Mistrust of the upper classes runs deep in the mountains, with good reason. During those bloody mine wars, company owners hired thugs and conspired with the sheriffs to keep the workers down. Miners were paid in scrip, or company money, meaning they could only buy from the company store. In that system, few other businesses could survive. And despite the caricature of coal miners as endlessly loyal to the industry, generations of boom-and-bust cycles have left them fully aware that coal may put food on your table, but it'll take far more than it gives.

A few weeks into the railroad blockade, local musicians stopped by to play Appalachian folk music for the protesters. One song was an old classic by folk singer Jean Richie:

> *I was born and raised at the mouth of Hazard Holler*
> *Coal cars rolled and rumbled past my door*
> *But now they stand in a rusty row all empty*
> *'Cause the L&N don't stop here anymore*

Coal mining has had a chokehold on Appalachia for decades. Politically connected coal barons lobbied against competitive industries and even mom-and-pop businesses, keeping whole swaths of the country almost entirely reliant on one industry.

But coal production in Appalachia reached its peak in 1990, and since then it's actually produced less of the black stuff than the Powder River Basin of Wyoming. Experts project the interior coalfields known as the Illinois Basin will soon overtake the Appalachian coalfields as well. The number of people employed in the coal industry just in Appalachian Kentucky cratered from 14,381 in 2008[1] to just 4,121 in 2018.[2]

"Friends of Coal" stickers still appear on the bumpers of a remarkable number of cars, but few of those cars' owners could tell you that the Friends of Coal campaign was paid for by coal industry groups that were simultaneously working to remove workplace protections, union benefits, and environmental protections.

The narrative that President Barack Obama was waging a war on coal was a political tool designed to leverage coal-reliant communities against environmentalist agendas. And it worked.

But Obama-era environmental regulations weren't what caused the decline in the industry. It was cheap natural gas, more affordable renewable energy, new methods of extracting coal that required fewer workers, and electric utilities responding to market trends and closing down uncompetitive coal-fired power plants.

For a lot of people, there's a valor associated with mining, akin to serving in the military or working as a police officer. Miners will tell you that coal mining is more than a job, that it runs in their blood. Now that economic forces are sending coal the way of the dinosaurs, some miners feel that they're not only losing a job, but they're losing a part of their identity.

After those first energetic weeks, posted up where the tracks crossed Sand Hill Bottom Road, the protest crowd began to thin. Miner Chris Lewis and his son Dalton, who was also a miner but had not worked for

Blackjewel, moved to Alabama to work in coal mines there. Curtis Cress got a job at a tattoo parlor for a little while, but the pay was too irregular, so he kept looking. David Pratt Jr. and his wife, Wendy, who had been a mainstay at the protest along with their children, both got into nursing school and devoted themselves to their classes.

But the protest didn't truly end until Chris and Stacy Rowe packed up and left one Tuesday in late September. Chris got a job hauling truck. And the pair had grown disheartened in recent days, since it was mostly just the two of them, scrolling through Facebook beside the railroad.

Finally, after months of negotiations with the federal Department of Labor, Blackjewel paid back wages to its hundreds of employees.

A few months after the protest ended, I checked back in with some of the Blackjewel miners I felt closest to. I wanted to know, after the dust settled, what it all meant, how those two months of protest had shaped them. Here's what Pratt sent me:

"It changed a lot for me. It changed my entire family's future, and outlook on big business. It also made me look at our local economy a lot harder, and wonder what the future will hold for those that stay here. If our leaders don't secure something for the younger generations, and my generation, for that matter, this place will be a ghost town."

The full legacy of the Blackjewel protest is yet to be seen, but it's already had a significant impact. Reporting from the *Lexington Herald-Leader*, a local newspaper, showed that the administration of former governor Matt Bevin had allowed coal companies to avoid posting bonds that could have helped miners get paid in just this sort of circumstance. And on January 20, 2020, miners working for a different company called Quest Energy pulled their own pickup trucks crossways in front of a different coal train, this time in nearby Pike County. Miners said they hadn't been paid since December 27.

"I just want paid," miner Dalton Russell told me. "Ain't I worth that?"

The miners occupied the tracks for three days, until a payroll employee for Quest personally come to the railroad tracks to assure miners they would be paid.

Quest's parent company, American Resources Corporation, told me in a statement, "The men have been paid, not because of their actions on the tracks, but because of the actions of all the rest of our team that have stuck together to make this company work. Their actions almost blew things up but because of the hardworking men and women that stuck together we got it resolved."

The Blackjewel blockaders may have created a new form of protest in coal country, but they also illustrated the limited options available to people in their circumstances. Their politicians did not protect them. Their bosses would not protect them. With no other way to advocate for themselves, coal miners had no choice but to put their very bodies on the line.

# THE YOUNG HANDS THAT FEED US

## An Estimated 524,000 Children Work Unimaginably Long Hours in America's Grueling Agricultural Fields, and It's All Perfectly Legal

### Karen Coates and Valeria Fernández

I t was the last day of March 2018, the day before Easter, the season of onions. By midmorning, sixteen-year-old Berenise had already loaded a few pails. She held sharp, rusty shears that demanded careful precision; one slip, and they could take a finger. Berenise worked alongside her ten-year-old brother, Salvador, and her parents a few paces away. Sunlight beamed across mile after mile of flat green fields, broken only by a few dirt roads. When it's harvest time like this, multigenerational families, from young children to grandparents, cluster among the furrows. The land is scattered with plastic pails, packing crates, and a few blue porta-potties. Onions blanket the ground, as far as the eye can see; the air smells sweet and sharp. Human backs form U-shaped curves, heads covered in hats and hoods, pants and fingers stained with chloro-phyll and mud.

This particular scene unfolded near McAllen, in the far southern tip of Texas along the United States–Mexico border, but it repeats itself, in field after field, day after day, across more than a million acres of farmland in the Rio Grande Valley. It goes on and on until daylight fades or the very last vegetable is picked and crated—whichever comes first. In this field, Berenise and her brother had developed a routine: grasp an onion, shake the dirt, cut the greens, snip the roots, toss the onion into a bucket; when the bucket is filled, lug it to a plastic crate as tall as their hips, hoist the pail, and dump the load. A full crate earned the family $16.

"If you work hard, it's good," said their father, Salvador Sr., forty-three, who was willing to publicly share most every detail of his life and his job, except his family's last name—because he and his wife are undocu-mented immigrants from Veracruz, Mexico. "The work in the fields—it's rough," he said. He had been doing it for the last three years after his work as a mechanic fell through; since then, he has worked the fields and taken jobs fixing cars on the side for extra cash. "If I had documents, I would have a steady job."

This job—farmwork—is a job that no one wants. It's the definition of stoop labor, and it frequently has life-altering consequences. "I worked like a donkey all the time," recalled an eighty-five-year-old grandmother named Juliana Martínez, who spent most of her life in the fields. She began as a child in Mexico, then worked for decades in South Texas. She felt no pain. "Maybe when I get older, it will start hurting," she said laughing. But she was lucky: among farmworkers, injuries are common, sometimes disabling, occasionally fatal. More than that: workers talk of astoundingly high rates of cancer, diabetes, Parkinson's, Alzheimer's, birth defects, and early deaths—and they all suspect pesticide exposure is a culprit.

Still, across the United States, up to three million people do this work (estimates vary widely; there is no concise, accurate tally of the total number of farmworkers in the States).[1] "The only reason they're out there harvesting those crops," says Juan Anciso, professor at Texas A&M AgriLife, an agricultural research and extension service in Weslaco, "is because they don't have an alternative." They don't have the education or job skills needed to pull them out of farmwork, he says. And the food industry, in many cases, has few alternatives; there are no machines to pick many of the most delicate greens, vegetables, and herbs. The work requires human hands. It's hard, monotonous labor that supports an industry worth approximately $990 billion—and feeds the nation. Many Americans, maybe most, don't think about that, Anciso says. "You go and have your salad but don't realize someone's breaking their back to harvest that." Most shocking of all, hundreds of thousands of these workers are minors—and it's perfectly legal.

It's actually hard to measure precisely how many children are working on U.S. farms (partly because different agencies use different criteria and different ages in their measurements), but a 2014 Childhood Agricultural Injury Survey puts the number at 524,000.[2]

There was a steady breeze that day in the onion field, which helped to cut the heat. Still, Berenise's brow was dotted with sweat. Occasionally, semis growled past on the nearby highway, but mostly the field was quiet except for the *snip snip snip* of scissors and the crumbling of dirt granules as they fell from the onions to the ground. Talk is time, and time is money—so words were scarce. But Berenise paused for a moment to say she was looking forward to Easter Sunday and a break from the fields. "We're gonna go to the zoo, the whole family," she said. "I haven't gone in a long time because my parents are always working."

THE NEXT MORNING, all across the valley, the fields were empty, the churches full. Just a few miles away from the onion field in the town of San Juan, the Martínez family—four generations strong—gathered for a backyard fiesta of chicken and rice, beans and salsa, and games of musical chairs. "No Rompas Más (Mi Pobre Corazón)," a Spanish-language cover of "Achy Breaky Heart," blasted from outdoor speakers. Juliana Martínez passed out eggshells she had painted and filled with confetti and baby powder. It's a Mexican tradition she learned in her hometown, and she's done it since she was six years old. Suddenly everyone leapt into action, smashing eggs on heads, leaving the crowd, the house, the trees powdered and speckled in a pastel rainbow.

Juliana was born across the border but has lived most of her life in Texas as a farmworker, then as a farmworker's wife (and mother of nine). She used to take her kids to the field, putting them in a little tent in the shade while she worked in cotton, carrots, chiles, and beets from 7 a.m. to 6 p.m. Back then, when the blistering summer heat of South Texas arrived, the Martínez family would migrate to the Midwest with its cooler fields. They'd follow the seasons, traveling north from town to town, picking one crop here, another there.

More than 300,000 children across the United States migrated to follow the harvest during the 2016–17 school year, according to the U.S. Department of Education. Each spring, beginning in March or April, many of those students leave their schools, moving with their families, packing just the essentials—sacks of beans and rice, a few sets of clothes, all stuffed into trucks that roll across county and state lines. As one worker put it, "Like the birds that fly, we go." Any child who migrates more than twenty miles is supposed to receive access to the federally funded Migrant Education Program, which aims to coordinate their studies at home with their schooling wherever their family lands for work. But many kids fall through the cracks. They don't finish out their classes at the end of the year, and they don't return until September or October.

Juliana's daughter María said that her father never saw the value of education; he saw the value of work. In her first days in the field at eight years old, she was given an ice cream bucket to fill with cucumbers for pickling. She earned money for her family and moved with them around the state, season to season. By the eighth grade, she had dropped out of school. Now, at fifty-five, María was a field supervisor for Rio Fresh, the same position with the same company where her father had worked. After nearly half a century in the fields, she was making $8.50 an hour.

"It's perfectly legal for children at the age of twelve to work unlimited hours on a farm of any size, as long as they don't miss school and they have their parents' permission," says Margaret Wurth, senior researcher in the Children's Rights Division of Human Rights Watch. The federal minimum age for work in most industries is fourteen; in agriculture, it's often twelve. But in many cases, children of any age can work. "There's actually no minimum age for children to work on their own family's farm." This variance is allowable because agriculture is largely exempt from the U.S. Fair Labor Standards Act, which establishes national requirements for wages, overtime pay, and youth employment.

According to the U.S. Government Accountability Office, "children of any age" may be employed "in any agricultural occupation at any time," so long as they are officially employed by a parent (or a person standing in place of a parent) on a farm "owned or operated by that person or parent."

Human Rights Watch argues that farmwork in the United States should be considered one of the "worst forms of child labor" as outlined by the International Labor Organization. The agricultural exemption from the FLSA not only allows children to work longer hours, at younger ages, than in any other industry in the United States, but it also allows children to work in more hazardous conditions, according to HRW. In agriculture, sixteen-year-olds can perform tasks the Department of Labor deems "particularly hazardous"; for all other industries, the minimum age is eighteen.

The United States is distinctive when it comes to child labor in agriculture. Wurth has done much of her research in Brazil, Indonesia, and Zimbabwe, and has found significant differences. "What distinguishes the

U.S. from all of these countries is just how weak the law is," she says. "None of these other countries allow children legally at the age of 12 to work as hired workers on farms. . . . It's kind of unbelievable that, in 2019, that's the status of our child labor laws when it comes to farming."

As a result, roughly thirty-three children are injured in agriculture-related accidents every day, according to numbers kept by the National Children's Center for Rural and Agricultural Health and Safety. A GAO report released last November indicates that children who work in agriculture accounted for less than 5.5 percent of all working children in the country during any year from 2003 to 2017, yet they accounted for 52 percent of all work-related child fatalities across all industries from 2003 to 2016. The report documents 237 such deaths among children in agriculture between 2003 and 2016—an average of roughly 17 fatal accidents per year.

Though health and human rights advocates decry the dangers of agricultural work for children, solutions are not as simple as banning the practice. For some families, the work is not only essential to their livelihood; it's also tradition. Families bond; children learn to contribute to their family's struggle to survive. But the agricultural industry has also learned to capitalize on this shared work ethic. The national minimum wage is $7.25 an hour, and most industries require overtime pay for days longer than eight hours, but many farmworkers, children and adults alike, are exempt from these conditions of fair-labor laws because some farms, typically smaller operations, are exempt from the FLSA entirely. Instead, farm jobs often still pay "piece rates." Onions: $16 per crate. Cilantro: $3 per box of 100 bunches. Collards and kale: $3 per box of 72 bunches. By law, those piece rates are supposed to equal or exceed minimum wage when factoring in hours worked—but they often don't, according to farmworker advocates in the area.

"Poverty is the determinant of whether a child is going to be working in the fields," says Norma Flores López of the East Coast Migrant Head

Start Project, and who chairs the Child Labor Coalition's Domestic Issues Committee. "If you really want to be able to get rid of child labor, if you really want to address the root causes, pay the parents enough. Give them a fair living wage."

**IN EDINBURG, TEXAS,** Reyes was nearing the end of his academic year. On May 10, at 4 a.m., the high school sophomore would pack thirteen pairs of socks, a half-dozen pairs of jeans and T-shirts, rubber boots, plastic pants, and raincoats, and he would start the three-day trip in a truck from his home in South Texas to Hart, Michigan, to work for five months in the asparagus fields and other farmland. He would be hand-picking and sometimes even working the soil by hand, breaking clods and removing rocks to prepare a field for planting. "I've suffered a lot, but you know what: I need to help my family," Reyes said. He was sixteen years old, his rounded childlike face transitioning to a young man's, with shaved sideburns and the shadow of a mustache. "If I don't do it, who *is* gonna do it?"

Reyes started going to Michigan in 2011, when he was just nine years old, accompanying his mother, María Magdalena, and her husband, Carlos, who is like a father to him. María Magdalena is still in the process of getting legal documents in the country, which is why she asked for only their first names to be used in this story. Working the fields is a family affair. "It's important to be together with your family," Reyes said, "to take care of each other, watch each other's backs." María Magdalena worked on a motorized machine, snapping off asparagus with her fingers, and Reyes walked behind, picking up any stalks she dropped or couldn't break off, throwing them into a box. "She was new," he said, "and she wasn't as fast as other people." In a photo from that summer, Reyes leans on a hoe. He wears a straw sombrero for shade and is bundled into an oversize shirt. María Magdalena thought Hart was green and beautiful but never got used to the cold and missed her parents.

The next summer, things changed. Just before they were supposed to leave for Michigan, Carlos had a dream: He saw Border Patrol agents detaining María Magdalena at a checkpoint, where officials found she was undocumented and deported her. The family goes three times a week to a Pentecostal church, and when Carlos told María Magdalena his dream, they decided it was a sign: God didn't want her to migrate, she said. María Magdalena, thirty-five, applied for papers on the basis of her marriage, but for seven years, she has been waiting because Carlos was a permanent legal resident, not a naturalized citizen, and the process takes longer. (Carlos became a citizen in June, which may expedite María Magdalena's application.)

While they wait, María Magdalena has been keeping a low profile. "Sometimes I try to drive. I put myself in God's hands," she said. "People ask: Do you have a license? Well, I only have the license God gives me." From Edinburg, you can't go more than about fifty miles north of the city before running into the Falfurrias Border Patrol checkpoint on Highway 281. Because Edinburg is within the Customs and Border Protection hundred-mile border zone, even going to dinner at a Mexican restaurant or getting coffee at Starbucks means that you could be stopped and questioned by Border Patrol. People live in fear of going for groceries and being deported.

Their worry is well founded. Before Easter, news broke from California's Central Valley that agents from Immigration and Customs Enforcement had arrested and detained farmworkers en route to the fields in the predawn hours. It's no accident that ICE targets the fields. Historically, agricultural work is one of the first jobs an immigrant takes after setting foot in the United States. According to a conservative estimate from the Department of Labor, about 46 percent of farmworkers are undocumented immigrants. "My parents were undocumented, and that's what there was—working the fields," says Juanita Valdez-Cox, executive director of the San Juan branch of La Unión del Pueblo Entero, the community union founded by César Chávez and Dolores Huerta in 1989. "The wages were so low," she says, "you needed the children. If we made a few extra baskets of onions or bell pepper or whatever we were harvesting, it's help for the family."

That's exactly the case for Reyes. The money he makes in Michigan each summer helps his family cover their household bills, because his parents' incomes are always inconsistent. Carlos mows the lawns in nearby parks and earns about $400 a week working for the city of Alton, twenty miles away, catching stray animals. María Magdalena occasionally works at a bakery making cakes for extra cash. Reyes uses his own wages to pay for his clothes, his cell phone—and sometimes Carlos's phone, too. "I never like being without a job. I never liked having my wallet without money," Reyes said.

But what the family earns is not enough. Their trailer needs work, the bathroom recently leaked, a car broke down, and Reyes's three-year-old sister needs babysitting—all of it requiring every penny that Reyes, María Magdalena, and Carlos can earn. Worse still, Reyes's grandfather, also named Reyes, is in need of dialysis but is also undocumented. For three years, the sixty-five-year-old's lack of insurance coverage has meant he can't seek the treatment on a regular basis. He must wait until it's deemed an "emergency"—only then will a nearby hospital treat him. So the younger Reyes has a special goal: to save enough money to buy a car he can use to drive his grandfather to the doctor. In May, he packed his bags and readied himself for five months of strenuous labor.

One night, at his kitchen table, Reyes sketched a picture of the machine that picks asparagus in Michigan: a tractor with "wings," where workers sit with legs outstretched, backs hunched, arms reaching for stalks to snap between their fingers as the vehicle moves through the field. Reyes said it's like trying to touch your toes, all day long. "And you are snapping, snapping,

snapping," he said, his hands making the motion in the air. It strains the fingers. But if workers miss a stalk, it grows bigger by the next day, and then it's even harder to snap. It twists your fingers. It hurts even more.

The worry and the work have been stressful for Reyes. Sometimes, he choked as he talked, struggling to catch his breath. In the summers, he said, he's constantly wet from the damp of the Michigan fields, and he can't shed the smell of asparagus when he goes home. It clings to his clothes and skin. He leaves caked in dirt and sweat and that asparagus stink. If he goes to the store, he might get stares from the other customers. "Sometimes we'll eat in restaurants," Reyes said, "and they don't want us to sit all dirty next to the people that are eating the food." So the restaurant host will seat the family in a separate part of the dining room. "We get it," he said. "But just try to be a little more gentle. Try not to judge the people that are doing your food."

**BY *DOING*,** Reyes means *producing*. Digging, hoeing, picking, plucking, snipping, snapping, lugging, and loading—all the sweating and toiling it takes to get a single meal to your plate. "We as consumers have a responsibility to recognize that there's a price to pay for what we consume," says Bobbi Ryder, former president and chief executive officer of the National Center for Farmworker Health in Buda, Texas. That price goes far beyond dollars and cents in the checkout lane. It ultimately affects the long-term health and well-being of those who work to feed America.

It used to be, according to food guru and journalist Michael Pollan, that food was politically "invisible." No more. The food movements sweeping the United States and beyond have made food justice into a topic of social concern. Their swath is wide, arguing for everything from animal welfare to sustainable farming practices, locally sourced ingredients to urban-grown crops, food safety to food sovereignty, crop diversity to soil health, water conservation to wildlife preservation, feedlot ethics to farm bill reform. But where, in that wide net of attention, is farmworker health and well-being?

Consumers will pay a premium for cage-free eggs, free-range chicken, rBGH-free milk, pesticide-free peaches, GMO-free corn. Labels tell us which salmon is wild-caught, which tuna is dolphin-safe. They tell us when our meat is "certified humane" and "animal-welfare approved." But who tells us no migrant was harmed in the process of securing our food, no child was deprived of an education to lower our cost? Andrea Delgado, legislative director for healthy communities at the California-based nonprofit Earthjustice, says we need a fair farmwork label to say, "This product came to you, and no worker was made ill or injured or poisoned before it got to you."

Some organizations are aiming for just that. The Washington, D.C.–based Equitable Food Initiative, for example, includes labor conditions along with food safety and pest management in its standards for produce with the EFI label. Since 2014, EFI has certified thirteen farming operations in the United States, three in Canada, fourteen in Mexico, and one in Guatemala. It's a positive step, but a small one. For the most part, farmworkers continue to be left out of the equation—at best, an afterthought—when their health and well-being should be central to equitable food debates, says Flores López of East Coast Migrant Head Start Project. Higher wages could make all the difference—but "companies keep trying to scare people: If we pay people a fair living wage, it's going to skyrocket prices," she says. "In reality, it's not. It'll be pennies to the pound."

Philip Martin, a labor economist at the University of California, Davis, has gathered research showing that farmers typically receive such a small share of the grocery store price (between 28 percent and 38 percent for fruits and vegetables in 2015) that even a sizable jump of 40 percent in labor costs would result in minimal increases to the consumer. Just $21 per consumer each year, based on 2017 numbers, would bring farmworkers above the poverty line.[3]

Without those wages, something else plagues many farmworker homes: "hunger," says Ann Williams Cass, the executive director of Proyecto Azteca, a nonprofit that helps families in *colonias* (temporary neighborhoods that can lack basic services such as electricity and plumbing) and rural areas. "The food insecurity is over 81 percent, compared to a national average of 18 percent." She refers to an October 2017 report, written by physicians (with the help of Proyecto Azteca) at Children's Medical Center in Dallas and Yale New Haven Children's Hospital, that notes a host of long-term conditions related to inadequate nutrition among residents of rural *colonias* in the Rio Grande Valley region, including malnutrition, obesity, and diabetes. The bitter irony is that, many times, the very fruits and vegetables that they are harvesting are unaffordable for farmworkers themselves.

Likewise, for farmworker mothers like Mireya, who works with her husband and children, Berenise and Salvador, in the onion fields, it's challenging to keep on top of meals for her children, ages two to nineteen. Most days, she wakes around 4 a.m. to prepare oatmeal for the younger ones before she goes to the fields. At night, she gets back as late as 6 p.m. She cooks something fast, but if she doesn't have time, she picks up chicken from the fast-food restaurant Church's and takes it home. Like many of their neighbors' houses, theirs is a perpetual work in progress, added to and improved upon step by step as the family accrues money. The kitchen is spacious, and the sink rests in a homemade wooden counter. The front door has no knob, the trim isn't finished, but many walls are painted. Berenise, her brother and sister, and sometimes her parents all sleep in one bedroom, the only one with air-conditioning. A couple of big mattresses are shoved together, one with a sheet, the other without. Salvador Sr. bought the land fifteen years ago, paid for electric and septic, and has assembled the house, piece by piece, ever since. His aspirations are obvious, but a lack of money constrains him.

Their neighborhood, like many *colonias*, is in a rural area far from any grocery store. So a lot of residents rely on corner shops selling chips, Coke, and other junk food.

"If they have a gallon of milk that they could have gotten at the grocery store for two dollars, the little drive-through is selling it for five dollars," says Amber Arriagas-Salinas, Proyecto Azteca's assistant executive director. "I know mothers that just don't eat, and they try to stretch every dollar." Local schools offer a year-round meals program, she says, and it's good that the children have that assistance. "But we should really be asking why the parents cannot afford to feed their children, and the reality is that we don't have well-paying jobs."

Maybe a slight increase in prices at suburban mega-groceries wouldn't solve all of these problems. But Bobbi Ryder and other farmworker advocates say it's time for middle-class grocery store patrons to start seeing themselves not just as consumers but as drivers of an economy, with real-world consequences. "It's not like any one person sets out to abuse another person," Ryder says. "Decades and decades and decades of practices and laws led us to the position where this is the population we keep perpetually in poverty." And yet, today's persistent inequities are unmistakable. Everyone must eat, but not everyone is forced to reckon with what it takes to grow an onion or to pick a beet or to snap a stalk of asparagus for the tidy, tied bundles in the produce section.

**REYES IS DETERMINED** to finish his education. He wants to become an architectural engineer and to build a better house for his mother. Most of all, he wants to break the cycle of poverty. In May, before he packs his things for the trip to Michigan, he meets with Roberto García, Edinburg High School's migrant counselor. It's García's job to make sure every migrant student in the school—some *131 kids*—knows what they have to do to complete their credits for the semester, or they risk repeating the academic year and delaying graduation. Roberto is balding, his hair turning white. He wears a suit every day and a silver ring with a golden cross. Many of the kids don't know that he started life right where they are now, so over and over, for years, he has told his students, "Never forget where you come from."

Roberto was born in 1951, the eighteenth child of twenty-one. Each spring, his family would migrate north to places like Michigan and Ohio. Some of his siblings were old enough to drive big trucks, and they'd travel in two or three of them at a time, with tarps in the back and six or seven families along for the ride. His father was a *mayordomo*, a supervisor of the fields. "The more hands he had, the more money he would make," Roberto said. This routine repeated itself each year, and on a couple of trips, Roberto remembers a time his mother was pregnant, about to give birth. "My dad would literally have to pull over and take everyone off the truck. And when we would hear that baby crying—*waaahhh*—two or three hours later, they would put us back in the truck, and we would continue."

For months, his family would live in terrible conditions, in barracks that were "infested with rodents" (though his family worked to keep their living spaces clean). Then, in October, they'd all return to Texas, after months away from school. Roberto's siblings were teenagers but still in elementary school because of all the school they had missed. Embarrassed, the García children stopped going to school—all of them except Roberto. "I kept on telling them, 'You know what, guys? Education is our only ticket to success. Mom and Dad don't have anything to leave us. We need to educate ourselves.'" It didn't work. Two of his brothers wound up dead at an early age—"because of drugs," Roberto said—and another was in prison for thirty-six years. "It breaks my heart to not have seen my brothers and sisters finish school the way I did."

In fact, most of the kids in his neighborhood in Edcouch, a town thirteen miles from Edinburg, didn't go to school at all, and the migrant program didn't yet exist. Roberto remembered that school counselors in his hometown discounted Latino students like him, telling them they were expected to join the military. Physical punishment from teachers and principals was the norm. Roberto recalled that bad weather meant "horrible days" at school because the students would eat inside rather than outside on the playground. The kids who could afford the twenty-five-cent lunch tickets would go to the cafeteria. Then the teacher would ask, "How many of you brought lunches?" Some of the kids would raise their hands. "How many of you brought sandwiches?" Kids with sandwiches could remain in their seats. "How many of you brought tortillas?" All of those kids were ushered to the back of the room, behind the coat racks and away from the rest of the class.

Today Roberto sees a lot of himself and his siblings in his students at Edinburg High, and he does his best to make sure they get their education. But old problems persist. "So in Georgia they were a little racist, so they didn't want me in the school," said fifteen-year-old freshman Charito Talavera. Her black hair was pulled back in a ponytail. It was October 8, and this was her first meeting with Roberto. "So they would say that they lost my paperwork. I didn't go to school over there for like three months. So when I did go to school, I was there for about a week before I moved," she said.

Roberto leaned over a red folder with her records and told her that he would fight for her. Charito travels with her mother and stepdad, but she doesn't work. Nationwide, nearly 10 percent of the 300,000 children eligible for the K–12 Migrant Education Program in 2016–17 were not enrolled in school, according to the latest numbers by the Department of Education. Their constant movement makes it challenging for school counselors to keep track of students' credits toward graduation, and kids often wind up in the wrong classes. Sometimes they skip school or simply drop out. The federal Migrant Education Program, started in 1966, provides funds to states to help identify and assist students who qualify, but it's not always easy, even with federal funding and the support available from counselors like Roberto. According to Texas Education Agency data, only 70.7 percent of migrant farm students who started in the ninth grade in the Edinburg Independent Consolidated School District graduated in the class of 2017. That rate is significantly lower than the graduation rate of immigrant students and economically disadvantaged students statewide.

Still, there's room for hope. Roberto loves to brag about a girl named Leslie Limas Treviño. Her family started taking her to Eldora, Iowa, when she was two months old. And because she only spoke Spanish at home, she arrived for kindergarten speaking no English. For years after, she spent half the year away from Texas, jumping in between schools. But she graduated in 2006, and went on to become a registered nurse. Leslie is thirty now and still travels every summer with her husband, who works in the fields, just as her parents do. They take their three-year-old son and five-month-old daughter. That's a specific choice she makes, even though the children can't work and they're too young to understand. "They need to know the value of things by knowing where everything comes from, and where they come from," she says.

When Roberto started in 2002, he says, there were roughly 5,000 migrant students in his district. Today that number is down to about 1,600. That change is noticed by farmers like Max Schuster, vice president of operations of Val Verde Vegetable Company, a multigenerational family-owned farm. Some of his workers used to bring their sixteen- to eighteen-year-old children to work on weekends or after class, but he doesn't see them as much these days. "The parents are kind of telling them: 'Is this what you want to do for the rest of your life? Or do you want to get an education, provide more for your family?'"

Roberto knows that's often easier said than done. As he reviewed Charito's red folder, he noticed she had lots of absences, and she was struggling in her Spanish class. But it was okay, he said, she still had time to make up for it; he would talk to her teachers if she wanted him to. Before she left, Roberto encouraged her to join the migrant club.

"If you don't do it, I'm gonna look for you, girl," he said. "You would be a very good officer in the club. You really would. I could see that quality about you."

IT WAS 6:30 A.M., and a sliver moon hung in the pitch-black sky over Berenise's house in Weslaco. A pickup truck idled in the driveway as Salvador Sr., Mireya, and their son-in-law prepared for another day planting sugarcane. This job pays by the hour, not the piece, and it's too dangerous for kids. So Berenise and the younger Salvador slept through the morning. It was the elder siblings' job to care for their two-year-old brother that day. That was part of their contribution to the family, Salvador Sr. said.

Salvador Sr. drove slowly through the dark, at times fifteen miles per hour below the speed limit. He'd been pulled over a couple of times at traffic stops, and he said he had always been honest with the cops. "I just show them my Mexican ID and tell them the truth: I don't have papers. But I have insurance on my car." He's been lucky so far.

By the time Salvador hopped on his tractor, sunlight illuminated giant clouds in a sky of pink, peach, and bird-egg blue. All around was a mash-up of urban and rural sounds: crickets, frogs, dogs, highway traffic, roosters, and radios. The tractor was hitched to a couple of long, rectangular trailers piled high with cane. A couple of workers hung an orange Home Depot water cooler from one of the trailers, along with a stash of paper cups.

A dozen or so of the most resilient men hopped atop the piles of sugarcane. Some wore gloves and heavy-duty hats, gripping long, metal poles with curved picks made of rebar, which they used to roll the sugarcane to the ground as the tractor moved ahead. One of the workers, Manuel Salazar, bit on a piece of cane and chewed it. It would later help to quench his thirst. He knew, by afternoon, it would get so hot he'd feel sick.

"The tractor jumps and jumps all day long," Salvador said. "But once you're used to it, it's a better exercise than Zumba."

Time passes faster with a sense of humor. Mireya, too, likes to tease her coworkers atop the trailer. *"Échele caña, Nicolas, échele caña,"* she said, urging him to keep up the pace. By 8 a.m., the sun was barely up, but the air was already hot and sticky. The humidity rose from the ground. The trailers moved back and forth, back and forth, hour after hour, across a field that seemed to touch eternity.

# IN RURAL COLORADO, UNDOCUMENTED IMMIGRANTS DEFEND THEMSELVES FROM ENCROACHING IMMIGRATION AGENTS

## Esther Honig

nside a mobile home somewhere on Colorado's Eastern Plains, the curtains are pulled tight across each window. Wrapped around the dimly lit living room, the peeling wallpaper read, "Live, Laugh, Love." A woman whom I'll call Ana has lived here for the last year with her husband and three young children. She and her family are originally from Guatemala and undocumented. On the afternoon we arrive, Ana's tied back her long black hair, still damp from a late morning shower. She explains that her husband was called into work at his job at a nearby dairy. Today's legal training—a breakdown of the family's rights at the hands of immigration authorities—will just include her and the kids.

85

While the majority of the estimated 10.7 million undocumented immigrants in America reside in cities, in the last twenty years, small undocumented communities have settled into rural areas, where they find work in agriculture. Rural towns offer a lower cost of living and an increased sense of security, but these immigrants may also find themselves isolated from legal resources and unaware of their rights. Like many people in her position, Ana fears she and her family could be discovered by immigration officials. When she learned they could receive training to protect themselves—in the privacy of their own home—she agreed.

In these small Colorado towns, rumors of potential roundups and ICE sightings spread quickly, driving families to stay home behind locked doors. Fear ripples through every corner of the economy: workers stay home, employers fall behind on productivity, and local stores see fewer sales. In July, when President Trump announced a week of mass immigration raids throughout the United States, Susana Guardado, the director of a community center in Fort Morgan, held an emergency know-your-rights seminar.

In this small agricultural town in the northeastern corner of Colorado, traffic in Fort Morgan crawls down the wide lanes of the main street. The downtown is an assortment of aging brick storefronts, many built during the sugar boom of the early 1900s. Today the local shops include a *Michoacana* ice cream store, a *panadaria* with fresh pastries, and the *las vaquiritas* for cowboy boots and jeans. Close to half of all current residents here identify as Latino and that includes a sizable immigrant population, some of whom are undocumented. But on the night that Guardado held her training, she was puzzled when almost no one showed up.

"People felt that if they were showing up to our building, which is a public entity, that they were somehow outing their status," she said.

In Fort Morgan, most everyone shops at the local Walmart or they go to the town cinema to see the latest releases. Residents told me the only downside to living here is that everyone knows each other's business, or at least they think they do. According to Guardado, it can't offer the same anonymity as a big city. To make matters worse, the community center is located on the town's main street, and, as in most rural towns, it's a place most people come to be seen. Perhaps for this reason people feared they'd be spotted by neighbors or coworkers and, as Guardado later learned, they felt it was as if they were announcing to the world, "I hold this status. You're seeing my face; you know my name."

In the end, the mass deportations Trump promised never happened. Rather than hundreds of thousands, only thirty-five arrests took place nationwide, according to government documents obtained by the *New York Times*. Yet Guardado was still determined to continue the know-your-rights training and rather than requesting individuals come to the community center, she decided she'd travel to them and hold the training in the privacy of their homes. Soon Guardado was driving farther into rural Colorado, up to one or two hours from home. Word of her training had spread among families and friends and she'd often spend her weekends, and her own money, speaking to groups of twenty or more, mostly dairy workers and farmhands, gathered in backyards and in living rooms.

Despite being only twenty-six, Guardado has a gentle authority. With her long dark eyelashes and youthful round face, she speaks to law enforcement, elected officials, and journalists with the same steady, even tone. Her hands are folded quietly at her lap. As the director of One Morgan County, it's her job to help immigrants and refugees navigate local resources, like how to obtain a driver's license or enroll in English courses. When she first took the position in 2017, she lacked formal training and says she didn't feel qualified. It was only later she realized she could pull from her childhood experience of immigrating to the United States from Mexico. For as long as she can remember, Guardado, who grew up in Fort Morgan, has been interpreting for her own parents and helping them overcome bureaucratic hurdles. Her role as a community navigator finally "clicked" when she began to ask herself the question, "What could my family have used when we first arrived?"

The job requires long hours and those weekend visits she makes on her own time are often to clients outside her official jurisdiction of Morgan County.

"Families should be together," she said. "How can we keep them together, what measures can we take?" she said.

On a Saturday afternoon in October, Guardado and Lillia Vieyra, a local volunteer, travel to Ana's home.

"The most important thing," says Guardado in Spanish, "is never to carry any false documents with you. That's a red flag in this whole thing."

Ana's children huddle close to her on the couch as the two women break down her "defense" strategy.

If you're pulled over in your car, don't lie to an immigration official, she explains, and never sign anything without a lawyer present. But what should the family do if immigration officials come knocking at their door? This part of the training is the "offensive" strategy. ICE agents may have found their address, explains Guardado, or perhaps they've come to the neighborhood in search of someone else but decide to see if they can find additional suspects. She warns them to be aware of any strangers, as ICE agents may wear plain clothes and drive unmarked cars—always ask for their identification. Then she shares what is perhaps her most valuable advice, which she'll repeat several times throughout the training. Under no circumstances should the family open their door.

"That's like giving them permission to come into your home. It's an invitation to come inside," she said.

The Fourth Amendment, which protects against unreasonable searches and seizures, extends to anyone living in the United States, regardless of their status. Only agents with a warrant signed by a judge can force their way into a private residence. Guardado explains that without a warrant ICE agents will say almost anything to convince the family to let them inside.

The Colorado Immigrant Rights Coalition has documented several cases of such abuse, including plainclothes officers who refuse to iden-tify themselves. Regional director Josh Stallings says that in the mountain town of Durango, agents told a suspect that while they didn't possess a signed warrant, one was "on its way right now." In a case last summer, agents promised three men that they wouldn't be arrested if they opened their door to answer a few questions.

"Once they were outside, they did end up arresting them," says Stall-ings. At least two of the men will be deported.

Not only do these immigrants contend with language barriers and a foreign legal system, but they must stand their ground even in the face of deceit and intimidation.

In her experience, Guardado says people tend to think of deportation in the context of mass raids—like the one last August, when ICE agents arrived at seven chicken plants in Mississippi and arrested 680 people suspected of working without authorization. In reality, ICE tends to keep a much lower profile by making hundreds of individual arrests on a daily basis across the United States. According to the agency, between January and March of this year of 2019, ICE arrested 685 individuals, more than 200 a month, from across Colorado. It's important to note that not all ICE arrests result in deportations, and the number of arrests has declined since spiking in 2018.

Tracking these individual arrests is far more complicated, which is why the Colorado Immigrant Rights Coalition helps run a statewide hot-line called the Rapid Response Network. Anyone can call to report what they suspect to be ICE agents making arrests and a trained volunteer, called a verifier, will arrive at the scene to attempt to confirm or deny it. The network then posts this activity in real time to a Facebook page, which updates thousands of followers who can avoid the reported neigh-borhood or grocery store if they happen to be nearby. In what can be a sea of rumors and sensationalized media reports, the Rapid Response Net-work has become a reliable source for communities who fear deportation.

Based on the calls they've received, they can also identify certain patterns in how the agency operates.

Stallings says ICE agents in rural areas tend to target specific locations. "There's been a number of times in some of our rural counties where ICE has shown up at the courthouse and arrested people. Either in the courthouse or right after they've left," he said.

While the majority of ICE arrests take place in the cities, Stallings says when they occur in rural areas the network tends to break down; often the closest volunteer is more than an hour away and by the time they arrive at the scene there may be few clues to work with. This means people like Ana are largely on their own and their arrests go unreported.

Inside the trailer, Susana Guardado played short videos on her laptop to help Ana and her children visualize these hypothetical scenarios. Actors play immigrants and immigration agents. The simple plots reinforced the same key messages: you do not have to open your door and you have the right to remain silent.

Guardado said training can often stretch on for hours as participants feel compelled to recount their own stories of close calls or interactions with immigration officials. "People really like sharing what's happened to them. Most of the time they'll ask, 'What could I have done, or what would you advise?'"

But Ana has no stories to recount and few questions for Guardado. Earlier in the training Ana confesses that she cannot read or write, putting her at a severe disadvantage. How will she know if a warrant is signed by a judge? Guardado says illiteracy poses a great obstacle for their training and tends to be more common among their Central American clients. She worries that in a moment of panic and fear, Ana won't be able to remember what they've taught her. She might forget to ask for an undercover agent for their identification, or maybe one of the kids will accidentally open the door. She could be pulled over while driving her kids to school, walking to the grocery store, or leaving the county courthouse; any scenario could easily lead to the family's swift deportation back to a country of extreme violence and poverty, which they fled.

Thoughts like this give Guardado a deep sense of anxiety; to imagine it could have been prevented. It compels her to drive for miles on weekends and after hours to give one more training. At the end of the day something as simple as a door is all that stands between a family and their safety.

# DOLLAR GENERAL HITS A GOLD MINE IN RURAL AMERICA

## In the Poorest Towns, Where Even Walmart Failed, the Little-Box Player Is Turning a Profit

### Mya Frazier

On a Friday in April, Bob Tharp, the mayor of Decatur, Arkansas, takes me to see what used to be the commercial heart of his town. There isn't much to look at beyond the husk of a Walmart Express: 12,000 square feet of cinder block painted in different shades of brown. The glass doors are locked, as they've been for fourteen months. "For so many people in this town, to have to see this empty building every day, they couldn't drive by without getting tears in their eyes," Tharp recalls. The store had opened on a frigid morning in January 2015, just days into his mayorship. "Pinch yourself and it is true," he'd posted on Facebook the night before. For the first time in a decade, the 1,788 residents could buy groceries in town. But the reprieve was short. The following January, word came from Wal-Mart Stores Inc.'s corporate headquarters, eighteen miles to the east in Bentonville, that the store would be closed within a month.

"You rascals!" Tharp remembers telling the executive who called to deliver the news. "You come to these small towns, and you build these stores, and you cause all the mom-and-pops to close down, and now you're the only ones left standing, and you want to go home? Why would you do that to our community?"

The Walmart Express had been a pilot store, the smallest ever for the world's largest retailer, designed to test whether a national brand with major supply-chain advantages could wrest a profit from towns long considered too sparsely populated. The answer, it seemed, was no: the company closed more than one hundred stores across Arkansas and other southeastern states that same day.

Tharp did what he could to turn things around, putting out calls to urge a grocer, or any retailer, to move into the vacant building. He found no takers for a year, until at last, Dollar General Corporation, which had operated a smaller store on the outskirts of Decatur's downtown since 2001, agreed to relocate to Main Street—and start offering fresh meat, fruit, and vegetables.

The Decatur store is one of 1,000 Dollar Generals opening in 2017 as part of the $22 billion chain's plan to expand rapidly in poor, rural communities where it has come to represent not decline but economic resurgence, or at least survival. The company's aggressively plain yellow-and-black logo is becoming the small-town corollary to Starbucks Corporation's two-tailed green mermaid. (Although you can spot her on canned iced coffee at Dollar General, too.) Already, there are 14,000 one-story cinder-block Dollar Generals in the United States—outnumbering by a few hundred the coffee chain's domestic footprint. Fold in the second-biggest dollar chain, Dollar Tree, and the number of stores, 27,465, exceeds the 22,375 outlets of CVS, Rite Aid, and Walgreens combined. And the little-box player is fully expecting to turn profits where even narrow-margin colossus Walmart failed.

Later in the morning, after I meet with Tharp, I join Linda Martin, a Decatur alderwoman, to do a little shopping at the existing Dollar General. First we swing by the slaughterhouse on Main Street, owned by Simmons Foods Inc., the main local employer, where rows of chickens sit in five reeking semitrailers outside. Then we head to the crest of a big hill a half-mile south and park under the massive Dollar General sign.

We're greeted inside the 7,300-square-foot store by a foot-tall chocolate bunny, one of a number of items sitting on a clearance table marked 25 percent off. Easter was last Sunday, so the bunny can be ours for $3.75. Pastel-colored single-stem roses are available for $1.50, and twelve-pack cartons of Mountain Dew are stacked, without price tags, under the table. Deeper in, stuffed shelves reach almost to the ceiling, resembling a Walmart in the days when Sam Walton's "Stack 'em high, watch 'em fly" edict reigned.

Next to an endcap arrayed with no-contract cell phones, the assistant store manager, Debbie Schmidt, is tidying an unruly rack of knit stretch pants and tank tops, some actually priced at one dollar. (Dollar General hasn't technically been a dollar store for decades, and only a quarter of its products sell for that amount today.) Schmidt is a cheerful presence, and though she's preparing to pack up the store for the big move to the former Walmart site in two days, she isn't too busy to greet each customer by name.

"These people are not in here one time a day; they are in here three and four times a day," she says. Formerly, she managed wire transfers at the Walmart Express, and she says she found out she was losing her job, along with twenty-nine others, from the news teams who showed up in the parking lot. "Everyone was crying," she recalls. "Employees and customers, they were heartbroken. We were family." She worked for a while at a Walmart in Bentonville, but "it was nothing like it was here," she says. "We're just closer here. We all know each other."

Martin and I peer inside the refrigerated coolers at the entrance, which have triangular yellow stickers on each corner reading "Putting Healthy Food Within Reach, SNAP & EBT accepted here." Inside are packets of Eckrich Deli Bologna ($2), Ore-Ida Tater Tots ($2), and twelve-ounce bottles of Red Diamond sweet tea ($1). In another cooler, Martin finds the green Michelina's-brand frozen meals she heats up for lunch at her weekly quilting group. She glances in dismay at the price tag of the Mediterranean Chicken Pasta—$1.50—then marches to the register, explaining to the cashier that she recently bought one for $1 at a Dollar General in Coal Hill, two hours away. That's also the price, she says, at the Bentonville Walmart. "They're so good," the cashier sympathizes, blaming the store's supplier for the extra fifty cents. "I'm not going to pay $1.50 when I can go to Walmart and get it for $1," Martin tells me later.

LIKE MANY RURAL TOWNS, Decatur once fed itself and shared its bounty with the rest of America. At the turn of the twentieth century, it had a tomato cannery and exported peaches, apples, strawberries, and beans by the boxcar from a downtown train depot. A population of 245 in 1915 supported two grocery stores and four general stores. But in the 1930s, blight outbreaks and insect invasions largely wiped out local orchards. The depot is now a museum where antique bushel baskets and poplar harvest crates hang from the ceiling.

By 1962 there was one grocery store left, serving a population of 400. Small-scale chicken farms had replaced the orchards, and poultry was the town's economic engine, thanks largely to Lloyd Peterson, who employed almost half the working population at his chicken farm, research facility, and plant (the one Simmons Foods now owns). Meanwhile, twenty-two miles away, in Rogers, Arkansas, Sam Walton opened his first Walmart, and the era of big-box retail began. Walton later wrote in his autobiography that his strategy was to "put good-sized discount stores into little one-horse towns which everybody else was ignoring." He apparently didn't think Decatur reached even one-horse status. Peterson, a hunting buddy of Walton's, asked his friend many times to open a Walmart there, but Walton's response was always the same: "Lloyd, that dog just doesn't hunt."

So Peterson finally opened his own version, in 1983, called Decatur Discount, just where the Walmart Express, and now Dollar General, would later appear—the past forty years of global economic trends playing out in retail form on a single concrete lot. Peterson's 17,000-square-foot Walmart clone was as much a form of charitable largesse as an attempt to make money. The store did sell some food, but most people still bought groceries from the local mom-and-pop, which cycled through three owners. Walmart's growing portfolio of Supercenters and Sam's Clubs in Bentonville was hard for local stores to compete with. "We couldn't get a supplier to give us a good deal on anything," recalls Michael Wilkins, whose family was the last to run a locally owned grocer in Decatur. "In northwest Arkansas, Walmart dominated everything."

In 2001, observing its population of 1,314, a national retailer finally started paying attention to Decatur, but it wasn't Walmart. Instead, Dollar General's yellow sign went up atop the hill. The new chain in town had similar roots to Walmart—established in 1955 in Springfield, Kentucky (population 2,000)—but relied even more on low-income shoppers and recessions.

That made it a good fit for Decatur, where chicken hasn't delivered much prosperity. The town's median household income is just under $35,000, and the poverty rate is 32 percent, more than twice the national average; one out of every five people needs federal help to buy food. Workers at the Simmons plant, many of whom are Latino immigrants, say they earn as little as $8.50 an hour slaughtering and cleaning carcasses in grueling eight-hour shifts. (Simmons says wages start at $11.50 an hour.)

For them, and for longtime residents such as Martin and Tharp, the Dollar General has meant a place to buy laundry detergent, shaving cream, and other basics much cheaper than the local operations could manage. It wasn't selling milk or eggs at first, but within a few years it was—and accepting food assistance cards. Wilkins gave up his business in 2006. Twelve people lost their jobs, and Decatur was now in line with two of the U.S. Department of Agriculture's criteria for food deserts: it's both a low-income community with limited food access and a rural area ten miles from the nearest supermarket. In 2010, Peterson's heirs closed the pharmacy inside Decatur General (the renamed Decatur Discount), the only one in town; two years later they shut down the rest of the store, too.

About a year ago, as stores were going under across the nation, Garrick Brown, director for retail research at the commercial real estate company Cushman & Wakefield, was searching for bright spots in the industry. For five years running, he realized, a dollar store had opened once every four and a half hours, an average of more than five a day. "They see a need and are aggressively racing to meet that need for low-cost goods in places that are food deserts," he says.

Dollar General's sales per square foot have risen steadily in recent years, to $229, but they're still far below the industry average of $325 and less than half of Walmart's. Their gross profit margins were 30.9 percent over the last five years, though, compared with 25.1 percent at Walmart. The dollar chain doesn't carry the big-ticket purchases—bikes, appliances—that Walmart does. It thrives mostly on selling low-ticket items and basics, such as toilet paper, that help shoppers on tight budgets get through the week. At Dollar General, a package of eight Pop-Tarts is $2, or 25¢ a tart. At Walmart, shoppers can buy the same eight-pack, but more often they save by spending $9.98 for a bulk package of 48—only 20¢ a tart. Dollar General doesn't offer much bulk. A Dollar General store also has lower start-up costs; it spends as little as $250,000 for a new store, versus the more than $15 million Walmart puts into a new Supercenter.

The company declined to comment for this story, but in March 2016, Chief Executive Officer Todd Vasos outlined the chain's "2020 Vision" for 125 investors gathered at a hotel in Nashville, south of the headquarters in suburban Goodlettsville, Tennessee. (Shareholders include T. Rowe Price Associates, the Singapore sovereign wealth fund GIC, BlackRock, and Vanguard Group.) The presentation detailed a site-selection strategy focused on small towns, dubbed "Anytown, USA." Then Jim Thorpe, Dollar General's chief merchandising officer at the time, defined the core customer for the investors: "Our Best Friends Forever"—an extremely cash-strapped demographic, with a household income less than $35,000, and reliant on government assistance, that shops at Dollar General to "stretch budgets." Thorpe said these BFFs represented 21 percent of the chain's shoppers and 43 percent of its sales. His final slide touted a goal of increasing sales 50 percent, to $30 billion, by 2020.

There are really only two ways brick-and-mortar retailers can meet such a grand goal: open hundreds of stores or, much harder, radically increase same-store sales. Vasos's presentation included a map that looks similar to an epidemiological forecast, with yellow and green dots spreading like a pox. The yellow dots represented the chain's 12,483 existing stores. The 13,000 green dots were the "remaining opportunities"—some in low-income urban neighborhoods, but most in small and very small towns. There's almost no white space east of the Mississippi, except for the tip of Maine and southernmost end of Florida. The Rust Belt is overflowing with green dots piled upon yellow, and the eastern seaboard is almost exclusively green.

Dollar General's chief rival, Dollar Tree Inc., which also owns Family Dollar, has a plan that's almost as ambitious. In a recent Securities and Exchange Commission filing, Dollar Tree indicated that it believes the U.S. market can support 10,000 Dollar Trees and 15,000 Family Dollars. That's almost 11,000 more stores than its current 14,500, though it isn't putting a timeline on the expansion. In August, Randy Guiler, vice president for investor relations at Dollar Tree, told me it would "determine each year what our pace of growth will be."

"It reminds me of a craps table," Brown, the commercial real estate analyst, says. "Essentially what the dollar stores are betting on, in a large way, is that we are going to have a permanent underclass in America. It's based on the concept that the jobs went away, and the jobs are never coming back, and that things aren't going to get better in any of these places."

The dollar chains do provide jobs of their own, of course. The chain employs about 121,000 people nationwide and has said it will hire 10,000 more employees this year. But those jobs will be or are mostly low-wage. Salaried managers can earn about $40,000, but they often work long hours without overtime pay. These few positions won't make much of a dent in the fortunes of communities such as Decatur. The only new employment opportunities in the foreseeable future, other than at the larger Dollar General, are on the grim, hazardous industrial meat lines at Simmons. The company recently announced plans to build an expanded factory two miles outside town by 2019 and close part of the existing one. Tharp doesn't know if the city will lose its water and sewer contract with Simmons and is worried about the potential loss of tax revenue for the schools.

INSIDE THE CITY BUILDING, an old schoolhouse, Mayor Tharp, wearing a shirt with his name embroidered on one side and a paw print of the town's bulldog mascot on the other, takes a seat at a wide wooden table with Jaeger Bauer, an eleven-year-old from Cub Scout Pack 3410. Bauer is earning his merit badge in citizenship. He opens the discussion by expressing concern about how much energy the town's digital library sign uses. "The city should buy a solar panel," he suggests. After Tharp promises to check into it, Bauer asks what being mayor involves. Tharp explains that he had a rough start to his tenure. "I was purely aggravated and angry with Walmart," he says. "But we have to forgive and forget and move on."

It's a touchy subject. Like many townspeople, the Bauers survive on a paycheck from Walmart. They moved to the area from Texas twelve years ago, when Jaeger's dad was hired for an IT position at the Bentonville headquarters. His mother, Brandi, who homeschools her two children, still talks nostalgically about the year she was able to "shop locally at our company."

Tharp explains to Jaeger that he'd called Walmart every two weeks after the store closed. At first the company suggested he put a flea market in the space. "I told them I don't need another flea market. The town's outcry was, 'Find us something like Walmart, but with a pharmacy.'" When he tried soliciting other retailers, Walmart's asking price, $1.2 million, was too high. Over the summer of 2016, Dollar General had made a deal to buy forty-one shuttered Expresses, but the Decatur store was excluded from it. Tharp kept asking Walmart to lower the price, and by February, Dollar General closed on the Decatur property for $425,000. Even so, Tharp still can't bring himself to shop at Walmart regularly. His wife canceled their Sam's Club membership.

Later that day, I meet with Deborah Foresee, the school nurse at Decatur Northside Elementary, who explains that even before the Walmart Express closed, many families were struggling to stretch their food budget; the cost of gas to make the drive to Bentonville or another town with a supermarket is significant. The school relies on grants and donations to help feed students—districtwide, 79.3 percent qualify for a free or reduced-price lunch. After Walmart closed, Foresee heard about students eating processed meals almost exclusively and sometimes nothing at all. "So many of these families were doing ramen noodles or anything that they can buy in big packages and store for long periods," she says. In response, Foresee introduced a rash of initiatives: providing dinner during after-school activities, handing out fresh fruit three days a week, a snack-pack program on Fridays. "We make sure every kid who needs it gets food," she says.

Elizabeth Racine, a professor of public health at the University of

North Carolina at Charlotte, is among the few academics who closely study dollar-store chains. In 2010 she was asked by the county health department to study Charlotte food deserts, and she soon noticed how many dollar stores were in these areas. "It's not the kind of store a dietitian would love," Racine says. She describes feeling bombarded when she first walked into a Family Dollar—chips, rows of candy, coolers of soda—and wondering how places so filled with unhealthful food could possibly be authorized to take food assistance cards. "I've come around," she says. "I appreciate that they are willing to operate in low-income places because so many other stores aren't willing to go there." They may not be selling fresh fruit and vegetables, but they do offer some healthier staples, such as frozen meats, brown rice, 10 percent whole-wheat bread, and dried beans. She calls them the Whole Foods of Charlotte's food deserts.

Soon enough the Whole Foods of American food deserts could be Whole Foods itself. This summer, the U.S. Department of Agriculture (USDA) rolled out a pilot program to let food assistance card recipients order their groceries online. Ten companies signed on, including Walmart and Amazon.com, which recently spent $13.7 billion to acquire Whole Foods Market Inc.—but no dollar-store chains. The program could open the door for the big players to go back into very small towns in a way that lets them avoid the traditional overhead problems. But it could take a while. Dollar General's rural geography has an insulating effect, writes Brandon Fletcher, an analyst at Sanford C. Bernstein, in his May report, "DG: The Revolution of Rural America Has Not Been Televised," arguing it will be decades before Walmart and Amazon develop "a truly rural solution to disrupt the important role Dollar General plays in rural American life." That might be why the dollar chains haven't developed e-commerce strategies. Dollar General didn't start selling online until 2011, and Family Dollar still doesn't.

On June 3, a little before 7 a.m., Tharp puts a red ribbon and a pair of giant golden scissors with blue handles and "City of Decatur" engraved on the top blade in the backseat of his car. Then he drives down to Main Street—along with half the town, it seems—to celebrate the new Dollar General. The line started forming at 6 a.m., and when the doors open shortly after Tharp arrives, it stretches almost across the street to the farmers' co-op. The first one hundred adults in line receive ten-dollar gift bags; the first two hundred get goody bags with plastic Dollar General cups and samples of Tide. There are hot dogs, and Tony the Tiger shows up for photos with the kids. After the ribbon cutting and some introductions by the local management team at Dollar General, Tharp takes a deep breath and addresses the crowd. "We have a store," he says, "that's here to stay."

# FIGHTING TO BREATHE

## East Chicago's Struggle for Clean Air and Soil

### Brittany King

**W**hen driving down Interstate 90, in northwest Indiana, toward Chicago, the smell of rotten eggs is so pungent, and the smoke so thick, it's impossible to miss. The smog is as much a part of the East Chicago skyline as the small highrises that spike it.

I spent my summers as a child in Gary, seven miles away from East Chicago, and the exhaust from the factories didn't bother me then. I loved eggs, and the smell that permeated my grandma's backyard as I read or played with Barbies while she barbecued was more pleasing than dismaying. Of course, I didn't realize the impact the pollution was having on the environment and our community. Up and down the highway, to and from Chicago, the smokestacks pushed out pollution. And few questioned it, even my grandmother, who worked in the area at a local steel mill for decades.

Longtime resident Maritza Lopez vaguely remembers that the U.S.

Environmental Protection Agency (EPA) began placing flyers around the neighborhood, and ads in local publications around East Chicago, to alert as many affected residents as possible.[1] But few were moved to action. Lopez recalls signs cautioning people to take their shoes off at the door. Still, she says, "It seemed like it was no big deal. There was no talk about health risks, besides how it could affect children."

Many residents remained blissfully unaware of the severity of the contamination, and carried on as if nothing were amiss: their children still played in lead-contaminated parks and playgrounds; they kept their shoes on in the house.

That changed in 2016, when residents of East Chicago's Calumet neighborhood received a letter from Mayor Anthony Copeland explaining that they were living in a polluted area, with lead and arsenic present in both the atmosphere and the soil. Stressing the potential health risks, Mayor Copeland announced the closing of a city-owned housing complex just across the tracks in West Calumet, and local officials immediately began working with the Department of Housing and Urban Development to move more than one hundred residents affected by the closure.

Lopez, who had just purchased her childhood home a few years earlier, organized residents to demand answers from local government offices and the EPA about the extent of the pollution, and the dangers associated with it.

Three years later, residents are still dealing with contaminated dust and paint inside their homes, as well as contaminated soil in their yards.

## HOW IT ALL BEGAN

East Chicago, Indiana, was founded in 1883 and grew in tandem with the expanding lead, copper, steel, and rail industries. During the industrial age, canals were built and extended for easy ship access, and railroad tracks were laid. In 1906, construction began on a number of buildings that would later become the United States Smelter and Lead Refinery, in these parts referred to as USS Lead. The factory manufactured its own lead from 1920 until 1970, when it began recovering it from scrap metal and automotive batteries instead. All the while, lead and other toxic wastes present in the factory seeped into the surrounding residential properties, into the soil, into the groundwater.

East Chicago was once a bustling city—an industrial leader—where copper, lead, and locomotive factories thrived. Many of those factory buildings have since been demolished; others lie in wait, their windows broken, hungry weeds strangling their brick frames. In some cases, new industry has taken their place. Marathon Petroleum Corporation established a warehouse in the area, along with Marino/WARE, a steel manufacturing company, and Kemira, a global water treatment company.

According to the Census Bureau, 93 percent of East Chicago's population is Hispanic or African American. Almost 35 percent of the city's population lives in poverty, the median household income is just over $30,000—barely half the national average—and many of those who grew up here never left, the children and grandchildren of those originally lured by the factories at the apex of their run.

My grandmother, Angie Matheny, is among these residents. She has owned her house in Gary for more than four decades, and she began working at US Steel in East Chicago in 1964. Like many of the residents who still reside in East Chicago and in surrounding cities like Gary and Hammond, she had no idea of the type of health effects working twelve-hour days at the factory would cause her. In the 1990s, my grandmother fought and won her battle with breast cancer. Since then, she hasn't had many health scares, but does take medication to manage her thyroid and high blood pressure.

In 1985, the Indiana Department of Health declared USS Lead in violation of state law after it found lead particles downwind of the plant. By December of that year, USS Lead had ceased all operations and the Indiana Department of Environmental Management (IDEM) began testing the soil around the facility and other residential areas for further contamination. Working with the state and following the guidelines of its own Resource Conservation and Recovery Act (RCRA), the EPA worked with the responsible parties at the time to properly clean up the affected facilities.

Twenty-two years later, after further investigation of the affected area, the EPA determined the contamination had spread beyond the facility's original boundaries, and so transferred the responsibility from the EPA's RCRA unit to its Superfund program, which oversees the cleanup of areas that pose a risk to human health and the surrounding environment. Today, the USS Lead Superfund Site refers to a seventy-four-acre residential area in East Chicago's Calumet neighborhood, where some of the factories once stood and close to where Maritza Lopez lives.

The EPA has held more than a dozen meetings with residents, solicited their feedback, and collected samples of soil and groundwater in the area to determine the best plan of action for removing contamination in all three zones. The EPA's maximum level for lead content in residential areas is 400 parts per million (ppm). Most of the soil samples came back at 1,200 ppm or higher.[2]

The EPA office now addressing this site is the same office addressing the water crisis in Flint, Michigan.

## ENVIRONMENTAL JUSTICE
## AND COMMUNITIES OF COLOR

Although issues of environmental justice may seem new because of the recent spotlight on the water crisis in Flint, Michigan, and the standoff over the Dakota Access Pipeline, communities of color have almost always been the most susceptible to these issues says, Carlton Waterhouse, professor of law and divinity and director of the Environmental Justice Center at Howard University's law school.

"This is all grounded in the historic racial discrimination that we've had in the US since the beginning to the twentieth century," he says. Segregation and redlining persisted in the North and South even as America was also experiencing an industrialization boom. This segregation concentrated people who were already marginalized into limited living spaces, while white people had greater choices. They could choose to live in less polluted neighborhoods, to build their homes and start a family.

Communities of color found themselves near factories and industrial sites, not just in East Chicago, Indiana, but across the country in Michigan, Oklahoma, and Louisiana, where an area near industrial plants is actually known as Cancer Valley. By the time it was discovered that these factories were emitting large amounts of pollution to nearby residents, who were mostly low-income people of color, the damage had already been done.

Even when decisions were made by the government about how much pollution factories were allowed to emit, "those decisions rarely involved African Americans in government, nor African Americans in positions of authority at the companies doing the polluting," Waterhouse says.

The issues, of course, are structural. When working at US Steel in East Chicago, my grandmother recalls almost all of the wage workers being black men—she was one of the few women. Management were almost exclusively white men. "I remember when I first decided I was going to try working at the factory, I went up there with a few girlfriends of mine," my grandma recalls. "We thought there was no way they'd hire women, especially us black women. But they did, and so each day, I kept my head down and did my work." To this day, the executive team of US Steel is majority male and white.

## THE LEVEL OF A GIVEN THREAT

In 2017 the EPA ordered responsible parties to remove only the top two feet of soil, where the highest levels of lead and arsenic were found. After its removal, new soil will be placed over the top of older, potentially contaminated soil. When asked for feedback at a series of public meetings dating back to 2012, residents voiced concern that EPA's solution sounded like a minimum-maintenance plan.

"In public meetings, we have screamed 'this is a Band-Aid solution!' and unfortunately all the ground team can do is take it back to the higher-ups," Lopez said. "Expediting a cleanup that doesn't fully get rid of contamination doesn't solve the problem. I feel EPA has failed us in that manner. I understand they do not have the funds in their pockets, but they do have the resources to bring in the federal funds that we need."

Waterhouse explains that EPA's decision to only remove the top layer of soil in some areas of the Superfund site and not all is a common one.

"There are a lot of environmental challenges, so every problem in every neighborhood doesn't get the same level of attention and focus. For that reason, problems are ranked by what the agency knows about the threat and the level of it," Waterhouse says. This means that the EPA and other government agencies try to make the best decision given the information they have as well as the level of a given threat.

When asked in early 2019 about the chosen method for cleanup, an EPA spokesperson maintained that recontamination is not likely. The spokesperson explained, "The lead in the soil is not very mobile. Groundwater samples taken from four monitoring wells on the site only show low levels of dissolved lead, which are not high enough to recontaminate the top two feet of clean soil."

Lopez had her soil replaced in the fall of 2017, as well, but she is still concerned about the contamination inside her home, especially the basement, which can flood after heavy rains. In December 2018, family members came to visit on an unusually warm day. The unexpected weather caused the smell to intensify.

"They thought I was cooking eggs because the smell is a mixture of gas and eggs," she says. "Really it's sulfur from the surrounding companies."

## HEALTH RISKS

According to the Agency for Toxic Substances and Disease Registry (ATSDR), exposure to lead can lead to a variety of behavioral and learning disorders, especially in children.[3] Exposure to lead can also lead to hypertension and future reproductive issues for women. Exposure to high levels of arsenic can cause digestion issues, sore throat, or irritated lungs.[4]

During public meetings, Lopez has asked EPA and ATSDR officials about what is being done to address these health concerns.

"They just stand there staring like deer in headlights," Lopez says. "They know tests exist to figure out how some of our ailments originated. That's what hurts the most. Any medical [document] that says how lead affects the body, we have seen those symptoms in this area, but no one has admitted that or taken responsibility for it in our meetings."

Dr. Mark Johnson, the Region 5 Director for ATSDR, says agency representatives have reminded residents during public meetings where to go for blood testing. There are two federally qualified health clinics in East Chicago: Regional Health Clinic and HealthLinc.

"Adults who lived in East Chicago, Indiana, neighborhoods within the USS Lead Superfund site as children might have been exposed to lead that could put them at a greater risk of high blood pressure, heart disease, kidney disease, and reduced fertility," he says. "They could also have problems with their nervous and digestive systems. ATSDR encourages community members to talk to their doctor about any health concerns they might have regarding exposures to lead."

In 2016, shortly after Mayor Copeland declared a state of emergency for the Superfund site, the EPA sent letters to residents and property owners detailing the amount of lead and arsenic in their soil. The letters also encouraged residents to get their children's blood tested at the East Chicago Health Department, noting that blood testing was the only way to tell if a person has been exposed to high levels of lead.

But eighteen years before, the ATSDR had conducted a study of its own. In 1998, ATSDR completed an exposure investigation that tested the blood-lead concentration of children in the West Calumet and Calumet communities to the north of the USS Lead site.[5] The investigation found that 30 percent of children six and younger had blood-lead concentrations greater than 10 micrograms of lead per deciliter. The average blood-lead concentration in children is 5 micrograms of lead per deciliter, according to new Centers for Disease Control recommendations.[6] At the time, the ATSDR recommended the lead contamination be cleaned up. However, the Superfund site wouldn't make it onto the National Priorities list until a decade later.

Since then, residents say, the government agencies involved have focused primarily on children under the age of six, as if the contamination hasn't been affecting all residents for more than thirty years.

"I've been sick all my life," Lopez says. "My brother and sister both died in their early forties due to health complications. I've had tests done that say there are high levels of lead and arsenic in my urine, which means it's probably in my organs. So, the government needs to focus on everyone that's lived in this area."

Right now, ATSDR continues to work with the Indiana State Department of Health (ISDH) and the East Chicago Health Department (ECHD) to encourage blood lead testing of young children, particularly in the Calumet neighborhood. In February 2019 the agency worked with Great Lakes Center for Children's Environmental Health and ECHD to present a Grand Rounds event for local physicians and other health care providers to present information about lead hazards and the importance of blood lead testing for children. Additionally, ATSDR coordinated with other health agencies to set up a meeting with the new East Chicago Schools' interim superintendent, Dee Etta Wright, to plan educational activities related to lead exposure for children and teachers.

## KEEP FIGHTING

In October 2016, community leaders formed a Community Advisory Group with other residents to hold government agencies accountable and help residents stay informed. Currently, they're working closely with the Environment Advocacy Clinic at Northwestern University's Bloom Legal Clinic and the Abraham's Environmental Law Clinic at the University of Chicago. The clinics serve as advocates for residents, helping them parse through legal documents and demanding better treatment from government agencies on their behalf.

Since the group's forming, they've been able to get the EPA to expand its scope of work on the Superfund site, which allowed five hundred additional residential properties to have their soil tested; they pushed the EPA to examine drinking water, which revealed lead levels in excess of EPA's standards. Advocacy led to the replacement of some lead service lines; and lastly, the group pushed for dust testing and cleanup as well as lead paint abatement and were able to get the EPA to conduct additional tests that will continue through 2020.

When asked about moving elsewhere, outside of East Chicago, Lopez laughs. She is on disability due to health issues she believes are at least partially caused by the decades she's spent living within the Superfund site.

Although my grandmother grew up in Canton, Mississippi, northwest Indiana has been her home for more than fifty years. Her entire life is here, the job she worked for decades, her church, her best friends; they're all there. Like Lopez points out, it's not always easy to leave home, even when you should.

Lopez says if it made sense financially and medically for her to leave, she would have been gone. Since purchasing her house in 2012—before property owners had to disclose information about lead and arsenic contamination—her home has lost $40,000 in property value, she says. Furthermore, if she or anyone else residing in the Superfund site chooses to move, they'll be required by the Residential Lead-Based Paint Hazard Reduction Act of 1992 to disclose information about the contamination in the area, making it nearly impossible to sell a home.

"We've asked the EPA to call a meeting with the mayor, school administrators, and the governor because it seems like everyone is being told something different," Lopez says. "It becomes the blame game. I feel like we've been left to the wayside by our federal government."

Still, Lopez and other residents plan to keep fighting. Not just for their home, but for their humanity.

# FEAR

## How the NRA Sells Guns in America Today

## Elliott Woods

t was one of those gas stations close to a highway on-ramp in a seedy part of town, the kind that makes you regret cutting through the city instead of taking the bypass. I was pumping gas and trying to stay alert, sizing up everything and everyone around me. My eyes kept falling on a black man standing outside the convenience store. He was dressed in baggy jeans and a puffy vest, clothing with plenty of room to hide a weapon. Just a few seconds earlier, he'd nearly been hit by a car as he strolled into the parking lot. He had reacted angrily, slamming his hands on the hood. For a moment, something in his body language made me think he might pull the driver out of the window and attack him. But he skulked off, and now he was just hanging around.

The station was crowded, cars almost piled on top of each other, the ground covered in oil stains, the whole scene illuminated by sickly yellow light. Out of the corner of my eye, I saw a well-heeled young couple strolling past a Latino man who was leaning against his car.

"Why don't you gimme your purse," he said to the woman.

"What?" she replied.

"I said gimme the purse!" he said, lunging for the bag. "Give me your fucking purse!"

I raised my black semiautomatic pistol and shouted "Hey! Hey!" No one reacted. The three of them scuffled for a few seconds before the purse-snatcher reached for a pistol tucked in his belt line.

I fired. The boyfriend dropped. The purse snatcher turned toward me and I fired again. He dropped. Two bodies on the ground, the woman screaming. Had I just shot an innocent person?

"Put the gun down!" someone yelled.

I turned to find myself staring down the barrel of another pistol. The man wielding it was leaning over the hood of his truck, a few yards from where I was standing. I put up my hands and slowly crouched until I was kneeling. Then I placed my pistol on the pavement, half-expecting to hear a shot meant for me. The police pulled up a few seconds later and arrested me. From the backseat of a squad car, I saw them taking a statement from the man with the baggy jeans and puffy vest who'd had me on edge to begin with.

I was, in the words of National Rifle Association executive vice president Wayne LaPierre, a "good guy with a gun." I stood my ground. Now I was on my way to jail.

Fortunately, this whole scene, with its concoction of racial presumption and animosity, played out not in real life but in virtual reality—although I'm sure it occurs in various forms around the country all the time. I was at the NRA's booth at the Shooting, Hunting, and Outdoor Trade Show, or SHOT, at the Sands Expo Center in Las Vegas. SHOT is hosted annually by the National Shooting Sports Foundation (NSSF), a nonprofit trade organization that happens to be headquartered in Newtown, Connecticut, the site of the Sandy Hook massacre. The NRA rep who fitted me with the virtual reality headset told me that only about 20 percent of people who carry concealed weapons have proper training. For as little as $13.95 per month, I learned later, I could purchase the NRA's Carry Guard insurance, which would supply me with legal protection if I were someday to shoot the wrong person while standing my ground.

Carry Guard policies are managed by Lockton Affinity, a third-party insurance company, which severed its connection to the NRA in February, but this is some seriously effective fear-marketing, nonetheless. First, the NRA scares the mostly white people who buy guns into arming themselves against imagined brown-skinned thugs, in an era of falling crime— the overall crime rate in the United States is less than half of what it was in 1991, according to the Brennan Center for Justice; then it scares those same white people into worrying about their own inadequacies; and, finally, it scares them again with the prospect of legal prosecution in a country that the NRA paints as increasingly hostile to gun owners. Even if you shoot the right person, as it were, you still might be sent to prison or bankrupt yourself with legal bills.

Since the 1990s, the NRA has been enormously successful at stoking white Americans' fears about their darker-skinned fellow citizens while simultaneously cultivating paranoia about left-wing politicians seeking to take away their guns. Barack Obama's presidency was a watershed event in this dynamic. During his eight years in office, the NRA's membership grew from three million to five million. The organization's combined political spending during election cycles increased from about $6 million in 1998 to nearly $60 million in 2016. According to the Pew Research Center, the percentage of gun owners who cite "protection" as their top reason for owning a gun grew from 26 percent in 1999 to 67 percent in 2017. During roughly the same period, according to the Bureau of Alcohol, Tobacco, Firearms, and Explosives, firearms manufacturers increased their annual output of handguns more than fourfold, from 1.3 million to 5.6 million. Firearms imports also surged, from about 900,000 guns in 1999 to over 5 million in 2016.

What these figures reveal, perhaps not surprisingly, is that the fortunes of the firearms industry are deeply intertwined with the political activism of the NRA. And it is a worrying time for both. Fear of federal-level gun control is the NRA's strongest asset, and fear just isn't selling like it used to. The industry is in the midst of a steep decline that has come to be known as the "Trump Slump." Only a few firearms companies are publicly traded, so it's hard to track the performance of the overall industry, but most indicators, including requests to the National Instant Criminal Background Check System, which are required on most purchases, suggest that business was strong until Trump's election. Last September, the parent company of gunmaker Smith & Wesson released its first-quarter 2018 earnings report: Net sales were down 37.7 percent from the previous year, and shares had lost a quarter of their value. The company had to cut two hundred jobs later that year. At Sturm Ruger, another major gunmaker, the picture was equally bleak. Profits were down by half, and net sales were down by more than 25 percent. In February, Remington, which manufactured the Bushmaster AR-15 rifle that Adam Lanza used in the Sandy Hook massacre, filed for bankruptcy. "Nothing was worse for the gun industry and the NRA than getting Trump elected," Richard Feldman, a former NRA lobbyist and author of *Ricochet: Confessions of a Gun Lobbyist,* said. "I've been very nervous for a long time over the [gun] issue being the province of the Republican Party, and now we see it coming to a head, because the NRA got in bed so hard with Trump."

In response, the NRA has redoubled its attacks on the media and seized on the specter of "the resistance" to Trump to make sure that fundraising revenues remain high. "They use their media to assassinate real news," says Dana Loesch, an NRA spokesperson, in a video the group published in June 2017, narrating over b-roll from what viewers are supposed to understand as violent leftist rallies. Loesch, a TV-ready thirty-nine-year-old who ran a parenting blog called Mamalogues before launching a conservative radio show on Glenn Beck's TheBlaze, has become the NRA's most recognizable and vituperative celebrity mouthpiece. "The only way we save our country, and our freedom," she says in the video, "is to fight this violence of lies with the clenched fist of truth."

**AS A MILITARY VETERAN,** big game hunter, and gun owner, I had been aware of SHOT for a long time, but I had never attended. The year 2018 seemed like an opportune moment to get a closer look at the relationship between the NRA's rhetoric and the $8 billion business of selling guns. Given the NRA's resurgent animosity toward the media, and because, for the first time in the forty-year history of SHOT, the NSSF had decided to bar general-interest media, I chose not to tell anyone I was a journalist.

The show is the largest of its kind in the world, with upwards of 1,600 exhibitors. The booths, laid out amid 645,000 square feet of floor space and 12.5 miles of aisles, feature shotguns, hunting rifles, pistols, and every possible configuration of AR-15—the iconic semiautomatic rifle made infamous by its use in mass shootings—including a silly-looking zombie-apocalypse novelty model with a mini chain saw mounted where a bayonet ought to go.

Manufacturers show off their new hardware at SHOT and make deals with distributors and retailers who bring the products to the public. It is not an event of the type politicians refer to when talking about "the gun show loophole." The display guns are all nonfunctioning, and no money changes hands. You can't buy so much as a T-shirt. It is also not an NRA show, although when it comes to policy positions, the NRA and the NSSF are almost identical. "Given the obvious fact that the NRA's members are also our customers," wrote NSSF senior vice president Larry Keane on the group's website, the "NRA's and NSSF's respective legislative positions are often aligned."

• • •

**THE NRA OF DANA LOESCH** would have been utterly unrecognizable to the organization's membership as recently as fifty years ago. From its founding in 1871 throughout most of the twentieth century, the NRA was largely a firearms-safety and marksmanship-training organization. The NRA kept its members informed about legislation affecting gun owners, but it had no official lobbying arm, and it was a political nonentity. But with the passage of the Gun Control Act of 1968, everything began to change.

The Gun Control Act was a response to the assassinations of John F. Kennedy, Martin Luther King Jr., and Robert F. Kennedy and to the riots that were sweeping through the country, from Newark to Watts. The rising profile of armed militant groups in the counterculture movement gave urgency to the legislation. None of those groups caused more panic in the white mainstream than the Black Panthers, who had staged an armed protest at the California statehouse in 1967. The stunt spurred the California legislature to ban open carry of firearms. There was "no reason why on the street today a citizen should be carrying loaded weapons," Governor Ronald Reagan said on the day of the protest, words that would be heretical in today's gun rights movement.

A year later, the Gun Control Act created the Federal Firearms License system, which required gun dealers to be licensed and regulated interstate commerce in firearms, banning mail-order sales and creating a list of "prohibited persons" who would not be allowed to purchase guns. The blacklist included ex-convicts, fugitives from justice, and the mentally impaired. The bill also included a rudimentary background-check system.

The NRA had been embarrassed by the fact that Lee Harvey Oswald purchased the Carcano model 91/38 infantry rifle that he used to kill JFK from an ad in the back of *American Rifleman*, the organization's magazine. Testifying about mail-order sales, then–NRA executive vice president Franklin Orth said, "We do not think that any sane American, who calls himself an American, can object to placing into this bill the instrument which killed the president of the United States."

By that standard, Orth would have had to consider many of his peers insane. One of those men was Harlon Carter, a former border control officer from Granbury, Texas, who had served as an NRA board member since the 1950s. As a teenager during the Dust Bowl, Carter had gotten into an altercation with a Mexican youth named Ramon Casiano, whom he suspected of stealing the family's car. As the story goes, Casiano pulled a knife and Carter shot him dead with a shotgun. Carter pleaded self-defense, but a jury still convicted him of second-degree murder. The case would later be thrown out, but the event left Carter with a visceral commitment to the right to bear arms in self-defense and an equally visceral distrust of anything resembling government gun control. In a letter to a friend in 1969, he called the Gun Control Act "another drop in the water torture provided for good people by big government, without a particle of effect upon bad people."

Carter successfully fought to shift the organization's priorities from training to Second Amendment activism, and the creation of the ATF in 1972 drew even more NRA members into the ranks of his hard-liners. Three years later, the NRA formed the Institute for Legislative Action— an official lobbying arm—and made Carter its director. By 1977, he had risen to become the group's executive vice president, and over the next decade, along with his handpicked ILA director, Neal Knox, Carter would reshape the NRA into the hard-core lobbying organization that we know today, founded on his maxim: "No compromise. No gun legislation."

Under Carter's leadership, which lasted until 1985, membership rose to three million, and the organization became a formidable presence on Capitol Hill. But gun control would remain a marginal issue nationally until the 1990s, when a series of actions at the state and federal level accelerated the NRA's rightward slide toward the Republican Party.

Ironically, Bill Clinton and his running mate, Al Gore, were both seen as relatively pro-gun southern Democrats in the run-up to the 1992 election. Clinton even got an A-rating from the NRA during his campaigns for Arkansas governor. The piece of gun legislation that would brand Clinton as an enemy of gun owners was the Brady Handgun Violence Prevention Act, or the Brady Bill. The bill improved mandated background checks with law enforcement for all firearms purchases and paved the way for the National Instant Criminal Background Check System, which finally came online in 1998. The ILA vehemently opposed the bill, calling background checks an unconstitutional violation of privacy rights. Ronald Reagan wrote an op-ed in the *New York Times* in 1991 advocating for the bill, which had been in the pipeline since 1987—a level of Republican support that seems unlikely today.

But Clinton would bear the brunt of the NRA's ire when he signed the bill in November 1993, the same year as the ATF's botched assault on the Branch Davidian compound in Waco, Texas, which left eighty-six people dead, including four ATF agents. That November, the Federal Assault Weapons Ban passed the House of Representatives, after a spate of mass shootings involving an AK-47 and TEC-9 semiautomatic pistols, and a surge in urban gun violence related to the crack trade. Clinton signed the ban into law in September 1994, aided by a joint letter of support from former Presidents Ford, Carter, and Reagan. Both bills were short-term defeats for the NRA's fledgling lobbying arm, but they were also radicalizing events. For lobbyists like Wayne LaPierre, who had become executive vice president in 1991, the humiliation of the dual defeats was offset by their potency as red meat for fund-raising appeals.

In March 1995, the NRA took out a full-page ad in numerous national publications accusing the ATF and the attorney general of "stormtrooper tactics." The text described the ATF as a "bureaucracy whose mission is to make gun ownership by definition a suspicious act, and gun owners by class suspected criminals." Around the same time, LaPierre and the NRA's in-house marketing firm, Ackerman-McQueen, cooked up a series of notorious fund-raising mailers. In one, LaPierre wrote, "If you have a badge you have the government's go-ahead to harass, intimidate, even murder law-abiding citizens." Another accused the Clinton administration of giving "jack-booted government thugs more power to take away our Constitutional rights, break in our doors, seize our guns, destroy our property, and even injure or kill us." (The "jack-booted thug" mailer, close on the heels of Timothy McVeigh's terror attack in Oklahoma City, so incensed former president George H. W. Bush that he made a public show of tearing up his NRA membership. "Your broadside against federal agents deeply offends my own sense of decency and honor; and it offends my concept of service to country," he wrote in a public statement.)

The Gingrich Revolution in 1994 ushered in a gun-friendly Republican Congress and set the stage for future victories that would leave no question as to the NRA's political clout. Urban crime was reaching its peak, providing the NRA with an opportunity to capitalize on fears about drug dealers and crack-addicted home invaders. While the NRA started to push concealed-carry culture, struggling gun companies soon realized the enormous consumer appeal of handguns for personal defense.

Ten years later, in 2004, the NRA lobbied successfully to defeat renewal of the Assault Weapons Ban, and in 2005, it lobbied Congress to pass the Protecting Lawful Commerce in Arms Act, which put to rest "public nuisance" lawsuits brought by U.S. cities against gun manufacturers. Those lawsuits, which sought to hold gun companies liable for the extra policing and emergency servicing expense that resulted from gun violence, were costing gun companies enormous sums. Former Glock CEO Paul Jannuzzo worried about his company "bleeding to death with legal bills." The new law made it almost impossible to sue gun companies for anything that happened once their guns left the factory. Freed from the restrictions of the Assault Weapons Ban and bolstered by a congressional shield over the gun trade, manufacturers significantly expanded production of semiautomatic handguns and black rifles, among which the AR-15 has emerged as the undisputed king.

The NRA has never hesitated to use its fund-raising fear machine, with the gun industry reaping the benefits. Obama's tearful speech after Sandy Hook, and the renewed bipartisan talks of gun control that followed, presented an especially lucrative opportunity. In 2013, NRA membership dues grew by more than 60 percent, from $108 million to $176 million, and American gun companies manufactured 800,000 more rifles and one million more handguns than they did in 2012. The 2015 mass shooting in San Bernardino, California, had a similar effect, especially after Obama renewed his push for expanded background checks.

**THE GUN AT THE CENTER** of today's gun debate, the AR-15, is a civilian variant of the M16 and the M4 carbine combat rifles, which have been the standard-issue personal weapons for U.S. military forces since Vietnam. I carried an M16A4 for the better part of my six years in the Army National Guard, including a tour in Iraq. Late in my service, my unit switched to the M4, which was cool because it was about a foot shorter with the telescoping stock collapsed. The AR-15s you most commonly see these days are virtually identical to the M4. The only significant difference is that my M4 had a three-round-burst mode in addition to semiautomatic, which meant that I could shoot three rounds with every squeeze of the trigger instead of one. Soldiers rarely use the three-round-burst mode, though, because it burns through ammunition too quickly.

I knew that rifle better than the average teenager knows an iPhone. I could take it apart to clean it and put it back together in a few minutes, and I could put rounds on a pop-up target the shape of a human head and torso out to three hundred yards with plain iron sights. Shooting a small, high-velocity round, and with a buffer spring in the stock designed to absorb shock, the recoil is so light that you can place the buttstock on your forehead and shoot without getting a headache. That would be dumb, but you could do it. Try doing that with an M14—the weapon that preceded the M16, and which fired a 7.62mm round that was about 50 percent bigger—and you'd probably knock yourself out. Superlight recoil means rapid target acquisition and devastating rates of accurate fire. Add a 30-round magazine, or better yet, a 100-round drum, and you've got a precision killing machine. All these qualities, along with its widespread availability, make the AR-15 the weapon of choice of today's mass shooters.

ON MARCH 9, Florida governor Rick Scott, a Trump supporter and NRA ally, signed new gun controls into law in response to the shooting in Parkland, Florida. The Marjory Stoneman Douglas High School Public Safety Act, named for the high school where nineteen-year-old Nikolas Cruz used an AR-15 to kill seventeen students and school officials, raises Florida's minimum age for purchasing guns to twenty-one, requires a three-day waiting period for firearms purchases, bans the sale of bump stocks, and, controversially, sets aside $67 million to arm teachers. The NRA immediately filed a lawsuit against the state on Second Amendment grounds, arguing that eighteen-year-olds are considered adults "for almost all purposes and certainly for the purposes of the exercise of fundamental constitutional rights," and therefore should not be prohibited from purchasing rifles. Federal law already prohibits licensed dealers from selling handguns to anyone under the age of eighteen, but Florida's new law makes it only the third state in the country, along with Hawaii and Illinois, to raise the minimum age for rifle purchases to twenty-one.

The bill has largely been viewed as a politically calculated response to the increasing momentum of student protesters in Florida who are calling for an all-out ban on assault weapons. Similar student movements are spreading around the country. It remains unclear how long the energy of the youth protests will continue, but one thing seems clear: in the continuing gun control fight, the AR-15 will be the skirmish line.

Maksim Netrebov, a gun industry analyst from New Jersey, told me that after Sandy Hook, "almost every gun was sold out, and AR-15s which used to cost $500 were selling for $1,500-plus. That attracted a lot of people into the business, but by the time they got started, that boom was done and over with." Anticipating a Clinton win, manufacturers kicked production into overdrive and foisted large inventories of guns onto distributors, who passed them on to retailers on credit. "Now they have stockpiles of guns that are selling slower," and often for less money, Netrebov said, making it harder for stores to repay distributors and harder for wholesalers to repay debt from investment banks. "This is a deep phenomenon," he said, comparing the gun slump to the collapse of the housing market in 2008 and plummeting oil and gas prices in 2016.

As powerful as the NRA seems, it does not represent anything close to a majority of American gun owners. Pew estimates that 30 percent of adults own guns; with about 250 million adults in the United States, that means 75 million gun owners, and only 5 million of them belong to the NRA. It's reasonable to assume that a large percentage of American gun owners who do not currently pay dues to the NRA still support its views. But it is equally reasonable to assume that many gun owners are indifferent to the NRA and that others disapprove of the organization. Twenty-nine percent of gun owners think the NRA has too much influence on politics and policy, again according to Pew.[1]

Just as the gun industry has become disproportionately dependent on the AR-15 and semiautomatic handguns, the NRA has become dependent on a winnowing demographic of gun owners. Nationally, gun ownership is at its lowest point in forty years, with some studies placing the rate as low as 22 percent. According to research from the University of Chicago's National Opinion Research Center, 23.5 percent of Americans under age thirty-five owned a gun in 1980; by 2014, that number had fallen to 14 percent. Hunting households have declined by more than half in the same period. A Harvard and Northeastern study in 2016 found that 3 percent of the American population owns about half of the 265 million firearms in circulation. These "super owners" own an average of seventeen guns each, with handguns making up 71 percent of the increase in total guns in circulation between 1994 and 2015. The astonishing boom in the gun market didn't result from expanding the rolls of gun owners, but by convincing a small group of "super owners" to deepen their arsenals.

"When I look at our survey, what I see is a population that is living in fear," Deb Azrael, one of the gun study's authors, told the Trace. "They are buying handguns to protect themselves against bad guys, they store their guns ready-to-use because of bad guys, and they believe that their guns make them safer."

As a group, gun owners are disproportionately old, Republican, male, white, rural, less educated, and not wealthy. The NSSF and the NRA will tell you that minorities and women are fast-growing markets. But the demographics of gun ownership remain lopsided, and when it comes to the hard-core activist element of the NRA, the scales tip decidedly in the direction of cliché demographic markers that describe Trump's core supporters and the audiences for Sean Hannity and Rush Limbaugh. The youth movements inspired and led by the Parkland students are, demographically speaking, a better representation of the political and commercial future of guns, because they are a better representation of the demographic future of the United States. Not only has the NRA's rhetoric failed to scare them into begging for armed teachers, they're defiantly rejecting calls to "harden schools," and they're focusing their protest on inhibiting easy access to the weapons of choice for mass killers. The NRA doesn't seem to note the irony that young survivors of a terrible mass shooting are impervious to their brand of fear, or perhaps they do, and that's why they're getting more extreme.

At a time when the NRA ought to be thinking very seriously about its generational succession plan, it is entrenching itself deeper among the old guard. Research shows that young people were increasingly ambivalent about guns before Parkland, but the NRA's response seems to be pushing them toward revulsion. As for their attitudes about the NRA, a Quinnipiac poll in June 2016 found that only 19 percent of Americans aged 18–29 had a favorable opinion of the organization, compared to 51 percent of people 65 and older. Young, antigun activists are dominating the national conversation about gun control, outflanking the NRA and national politicians in a new media landscape that is their native terrain. Instead of taking these kids seriously, the NRA's proxies on social media and on cable and talk radio have mocked them, or worse, accused them of carrying out a "false flag" operation on behalf of Democrats. Conspiracy theorists have labeled them "crisis actors," suggesting that they're playing up their pain for political or personal profit. "The national press believes it is their job to destroy the Trump administration by any means necessary," Bill O'Reilly said in a quip that was sure to please the people who write Dana Loesch's scripts. "So if the media has to use kids to do that, they'll use kids."

In 2001, J. Warren Cassidy, Wayne LaPierre's predecessor at the NRA, famously told *Time*, "You would get a far better understanding if you approached us as if you were approaching one of the great religions of the world." The comparison obviously describes the members' zealous obedience to the leadership, but it also has a financial connotation. Churches are tax-exempt just like nonprofits, and in the church of the NRA, the gun is an idol, inviolate in the sanctuary of American myth. Its power to coax money from the pockets of the faithful is truly awesome. The rank and file donate generously to the NRA out of a sense of deep faith, and the industry goes along out of fear and financial self-interest; it is less like a partner than a well-fed hostage with Stockholm syndrome.

On the same day that I went into the Carry Guard simulator, I had walked over to where the NRA had stationed some of its policy wonks to field questions from the SHOT show attendees. I spoke to Daniel Sheppard, a grassroots coordinator with the NRA's ILA. I asked him about concealed-carry reciprocity laws—which allow gun owners in states with lax concealed carry statutes to carry concealed weapons in states with more restrictive regulations—and a few other hot-button NRA issues. Then I asked him about the drop in gun sales under Trump.

Sheppard laughed. "That's kinda the downside," he said. "We feel a bit of a pinch, too. People don't donate as much when they're not afraid."

# DOES STANDING ROCK
# LIVE IN YOUR
# IMAGINATION?

## Graham Lee Brewer

n 2006, a decade before protest camps were built on the Standing Rock Sioux Reservation, the readers of the *Fort Worth Star-Telegram* were asked to vote for the city's favorite work of art. The city's three largest museums submitted nominees, which included works by Georgia O'Keeffe and Andy Warhol. But readers instead chose an 1889 oil painting by Frederic Remington titled *A Dash for the Timber*. The painting depicts a group of white cowboys on horseback racing by, their hats bent by the wind and the feet of their horses stretched out across the dusty ground. A few of them are turned around, aiming their guns at their pursuers, a band of charging Indians.

Some readers wrote in to explain their choice, why they thought this painting was the city's favorite of 2006. "It fits our heritage better than all others," wrote one. Another commented on Remington's unique ability to truly capture "the golden era of expansion." This notion of expansion, what author John M. Coward calls a "mythical moment in the American historical imagination," is where Indians reside for most Americans. We live in your imaginations, your neatly constructed histories of this country, who made it and how. We are peripheral characters, an exotic glimpse of the past, the hero's antagonist, those who needed civilizing. Which is what made Standing Rock so irresistible to white American audiences. It was real-life cowboys and Indians.

But well before local and federal security forces began using concussion grenades and rubber bullets on Indigenous peoples who had gathered to stop the construction of an oil pipeline that threatened their water, the story of how the protests at Standing Rock would unfold began in government memos, meeting minutes, and court documents. The Standing Rock Sioux Tribe had been legally and philosophically fighting the Dakota Access Pipeline for years before the protests made national headlines. But digging through preliminary injunction motions and making records requests for government documents is something reporters who care about a community do. "It's the kind of work that an enterprising news organization committed to the principles of ethical journalism— public enlightenment, justice, democracy, etc.—could easily do if they had any desire to cover Indian Country," Tristan Ahtone (Kiowa) wrote in the *Guardian* in 2016. But when it comes to Indian Country, our communities are only important if they fit mainstream American stereotypes. As Ahtone later put it, "to make the news, one must 'play Indian' first."

In other words, Standing Rock only became news when Native peoples were being assaulted. The backdrop of the reservation's plains, dotted with tipis and a line of armored security, only made it sexier to the national press, but even then it took months for the media to care. A sovereign government making legal motions and impassioned pleas to pipeline representatives in council meetings to oppose an oil pipeline being built under their water supply, one that was diverted around several other communities, was not newsworthy. But Indians fighting cowboys was. "Horseback riders, their faces streaked in yellow and black paint, led the procession out of their tepee-dotted camp," the *New York Times* led with in August, months after the physical protests began, describing "a new kind of battlefield, between a pipeline and American Indians." Bloomberg led its coverage of the ongoing court battle over the pipeline with "the dark prophecy of a 'terrible black snake'" feared by a "Sioux Indian tribe." Meanwhile, the *Washington Post* was calling Native Americans across the country to ask whether or not the racial slur their football team was named after was offensive.

But soon the story exploded. It was sexy, colorful, woke, and maybe even, to some, romantic. The coverage largely fit into what Canadian journalist and professor Duncan McCue (Anishanaabe) calls the WD4 rule for how Indians make the news: Indigenous peoples in the media are typically either a warrior, dancing, drumming, drunk, or dead. And like much of the coverage of Indian Country by non-Native outlets and reporters, the reporting on Standing Rock lacked almost any historical context. As author David Treuer (Leech Lake Ojibwe) told *On the Media*'s Brooke Gladstone in 2018, the media all but ignored the federal government's own failure to honor its treaty obligations, setting up the events that unfolded at Standing Rock.

"The original sin is that the government broke its treaty obligations and promises to the Standing Rock and other Lakota tribes, which resulted in opening up of Lakota lands to private non-Native ownership; that's what allowed the pipeline to go through, because our government will bend over backwards for private enterprise," Treuer said. "To me, this is a story of local communities against capitalism, not cowboys versus Indians."

In his book, *The Heartbeat of Wounded Knee*, Treuer explains that American historians, authors, and journalists have always framed Native Americans as a once-great people, their glory long behind them. A people whose existence must be sacrificed for American progress. "The country begins with Indians but ends with Americans; there is no sense that they can coexist." Colonialism is not just an event in our past, it is the structure we live in today. The story of what happened along that pipeline cannot be told without the historical context of the colonial settler state or the importance of tribal sovereignty.

As author Nick Estes (Lower Brule Sioux Tribe) wrote in his book about Standing Rock, *Our History Is the Future*, to those who call the reservation home, the history and the land are the same. It is what cradles the bones of their ancestors. "For others however the earth had to be tamed and dominated by a plow or drilled for profit. Because Native people remain barriers to capitalist development, their bodies needed to be removed—both from *beneath* and from *atop* the soil—therefore eliminating their rightful relationship *with* the land."

As Estes points out, the Dakota Access Pipeline (named for the very people it was endangering) would disturb 380 archeological sites, including burials, and the point at which it crossed the Missouri River was the same place where more than 150 years earlier, ancestors fled the slaughter of four hundred Lakotas and Dakotas at the hands of U.S. generals. Others still remembered being forced out of their homes in the winter by the Army Corps of Engineers in the 1950s and 1960s so that the area could be flooded to build a dam that would provide power to places like Minneapolis and Chicago. DAPL was more than a threat to the Standing Rock's drinking water; it was also a threat on their sovereignty. Those deeper narratives are rarely of use to national reporters who parachute into Indian Country, extract a story of "plight" or "trauma," and leave, to return only if another tragedy occurs.

Whether it was in the racist depictions of Indigenous peoples in *Harper's Magazine* or the heartless coverage by newspapers of the genocide against them, American journalism has always helped maintain the existing order of colonialism through its representations of Indigenous peoples as lesser than, inferior, antiquated, ignorant, savage, or simply "not like us." Shortly after federal authorities murdered Sitting Bull in

1890, L. Frank Baum, the author of *The Wonderful Wizard of Oz*, penned a newspaper editorial stating that Americans' only hope for a safe country was "the total extermination of Indians. Having wronged them for centuries we had better, in order to protect our civilization, follow it up by one more wrong and wipe these untamed and untamable creatures from the face of the earth."

Those tired narratives of cowboys versus Indians, Manifest Destiny, the "golden era of expansion," and the disappearing Indian persist in the minds of Americans. And just like Remington's dash for the timber, Standing Rock was a story that American journalism helped create. Meanwhile, Indigenous journalists, from Kiowa pictorial record keepers like Silverhorn to founders of the *Cherokee Phoenix* newspaper in 1821 like Elias Boudinot, have been documenting the true histories of their people for lifetimes. Likely for most Americans, the idea that Native mascots are racist and damaging is a relatively new one, but journalists like Tim Giago (Oglala Lakota), the founder of Indian Country Today and a founding member of the Native American Journalists Association, have been writing about it for nearly half a century. And as Indigenous journalists who covered Standing Rock have pointed out, were it not for the inception of social media platforms like Facebook Live, a true sense of what was happening on the ground would otherwise have been largely unattainable to those watching from afar.

Ignoring these important voices is a continuation of Indigenous erasure, and it allows mainstream American media to act as a venue for exploitation colonialism. Stories are a resource to Indigenous communities, and to take and distort them for largely non-Native audiences is akin to the extraction industries. That kind of coverage does not help Native peoples, in fact it harms them by furthering racist stereotypes and myths. In order to properly understand Indigenous communities, reporters and readers alike should be asking questions about how colonialism has physically and philosophically shaped the landscape, where the Native voices are, and whose land they are standing on. And editors and publishers should be asking themselves if their newsroom is part of the problem. Less than one half of one percent of newsroom employees are Indigenous.

If we take a broader look at the Standing Rock Sioux, American audiences know next to nothing about this vibrant, resilient community outside of what took place on their reservation just a few years ago. I doubt many readers of this know the Standing Rock for the profitable food processing and telemarketing industries that help them maintain economic independence, the names of their artists or writers, or what they mean to the land, as well as what the land means to them. They, like most of us, live in your imagination. When we look back at what unfolded there in this last decade, there are other questions we should all be asking ourselves. What is happening there today? Do you care?

# WHITE WORKING-CLASS GRIEVANCE AND THE BLACK MIDWESTERNER

## Tamara Winfrey-Harris

As I write, the 2020 presidential election is looming, and cable news is flush with pundits pontificating about what will fly with folks in the flyover states. American political and cultural analysis relies on a specific understanding of the Midwest—small towns, American flags, country music, conservatism. Whiteness. The pundits are not talking about me, a Black woman born, raised, and now living in Indiana. Some 7 million Black midwesterners remain lost behind a biased and stingy narrative. Our importance as voters is ignored and our existence as canaries in the economic coal mine is overlooked.

This election season, of course, is no different than the ones that have preceded it. After the 2016 election, it was common to hear that economic anxiety—not a willingness to embrace racist rhetoric and policies—drove the white workers of Ohio, Michigan, and Wisconsin to cast their lot with Donald J. Trump. It's an argument that only makes sense if you pretend

Black people don't exist in the middle of the country. A majority of white voters in Ohio, Michigan, and Wisconsin chose Donald Trump (62 percent, 57 percent, and 53 percent, respectively), while only 6 percent to 8 percent of their Black neighbors did. What about the profound economic insecurity of Black midwesterners, a vast majority of whom were unwilling to bet on the promises of a David Duke–endorsed candidate to bring the local factory back?

In the case of the election that brought America's forty-fifth president to power, political analysis that rests on the idea of a whites-only heartland has kept us from interrogating the extent to which white citizens of this country are comfortable with—or even energized by—racism. And in a race allegedly defined by citizens' economic vulnerability, it erases the contributions of a significant portion of the American workforce.

There are more Black people in the Midwest than in the Northeast or the West.[1] Indiana alone was home to more than 60 Black settlements before the Civil War.[2] Most of us are products of the Great Migration, the exodus of some six million Black Americans from the South from 1916 to 1970. We came here to work, drawn by the industry of the Midwestern Rust Belt. We came here to escape racial terrorism, and to seek equal opportunity.

My maternal grandfather was among the more than one million Black migrants to the Chicago metropolitan area, attracted by the steel mills that give the South Shore of Lake Michigan its distinctive skyline. With a tenth-grade education, he followed his brothers and sisters north from rural Alabama and found a job. After working at Inland Steel for more than forty years, he retired with a pension, having purchased a neat little bungalow and having sent three of four children to college.

In my hometown, Gary, Indiana, in the 1960s, you could graduate from high school on Friday and be employed at US Steel by the following Monday. My father, a school administrator and Mississippi transplant who sometimes worked at the mill in the summer, says of the time, "If you didn't have a job, you didn't want a job." This reality dissolved along with the steel industry. The US Steel Gary Works employed some 30,000 people in the 1970s; by 2015, it employed around 5,000.[3]

The people in Gary, which is more than 80 percent Black, and in Detroit, another predominantly Black city, where millions of Black southern migrants once thrived making America's convertibles and Coupe de Villes, are rendered invisible by the country's racially biased understanding of the Midwest and the working class.

The so-called flyover states have long been an avatar for the "real" America—undiluted and undisturbed whiteness. It is that mythologized heartland that pundits seem to think will engender empathy, not the Black families of Milwaukee; the majority-Latino community of Dodge City, Kansas; the Burmese Chin refugees of Indianapolis; or the strong Arab community of metropolitan Detroit.

Black workers in the Midwest are as much victims of the postindustrial age as are white Ohio coal miners. Indeed, they may be feeling a deeper ache. Black workers with high school diplomas make less than white workers with the same education; the Black poverty rate is higher; and the median wealth of white households is ten times that of Black households.[4]

The Midwest is also ground zero for America's racial wealth gap. White workers are suffering, but their black counterparts are suffering more. A study released in fall 2019 by the Iowa Policy Project, Policy Matters Ohio, Center of Wisconsin Strategy (COWS), and the Economic Analysis and Research Network (EARN) found that in the "Midwest racial disparities in economic opportunity and economic outcomes are wider than they are in other regions, and policy interventions designed to close those gaps are meager." A 2018 report by 24/7 Wall Street revealed the fifty American cities where the racial wealth gap was most chasmic. The list was littered with Midwestern cities. The worst—Waterloo, Iowa, where Black residents make up 7 percent of the population; earn less than 47 percent of what their white neighbors do; are far more likely to be unemployed; and are less likely to own a home. A narrative that does not include, if not center on, the good Black folks of Waterloo, Iowa, makes our political analysis puny and unreliable. And the persistent political emphasis on aggrieved white men implies that some Midwestern families deserve economic stability more than others.

It is not just the white working class that is suffering—it is the working class, period. And we can't solve the problem if we refuse to see who those workers actually are. By 2032, according to the Economic Policy Institute, the American working class will be made up mostly of people of color, including Black workers.[5]

Cogent political analysis that understands America and its challenges requires seeing both the working class and Black America in their fullness and recognizing where they intersect. It requires acknowledging the experiences of Black midwesterners, even when this means adding unflattering nuance to the stories we've long been told about their white neighbors. Because without centuries of economic and cultural contributions from Black people in flyover states, America would not be America at all.

# RACE HOME

## Fitale Wari

In late August 2016, about five minutes from my house, Kenneth Walker, the only black volunteer firefighter in North Tonawanda, New York, received a racist threat in the mail. It read:

NIGGERS ARE NOT ALLOWED TO BE FIREFIGHT-
ERS. NO ONE WANTS YOU IN THIS CITY. YOU HAVE
UNTIL THE END OF THE WEEK TO RESIGN YOUR
POSITION OR YOU WILL REGRET IT……..NIGGER.

The following morning, Walker's house was set on fire—by a neighbor, as it turns out—and he and his family lost everything.[1] Shortly after, incredulous neighbors, the Gratwick Hose Fire Company, and town members collaborated to host a donation drive to help the Walker family. Others started a GoFundMe page.

I did not learn about this until I returned home from college over Thanksgiving. At the time, I assumed wrongly that the fund-raiser was minor, with only a few attendees. I wondered who participated, who idly watched, and who did nothing. I wondered what their races were, and if others noted their color.

**IT WAS JUST BEFORE** my junior year of college when I picked my dad up from work one still, humid evening. We reminisced about the past thirteen weeks of summer spent together, and anticipated the change ahead of us, on our drive home.

We were stopped at a red light, and I was deep in thought. I looked over at my dad, whose grip tightened around the door handle as he stared to his right.

Two men in a red Chevy Silverado were inspecting us. The truck had pulled out of the Key Bank drive-through and slowly eased out onto the road, rolling to a stop next to us. The driver revved the engine as two Confederate flags thrashed in the wind.

I searched my dad's face. He focused on the rusted-out truck while I silently willed the light to change.

**THE SMELL OF CIGARETTES** and stale beer suffuse the neighborhood as truckers and motorcycle gangs crawl from bar to bar on Sunday nights. High schoolers sneak out of their houses to test their fake IDs and pick fights. You can hear factory workers shouting profanities as they slap their beer bellies together. This is classic North Tonawanda.

One of my dad's friends has lived in North Tonawanda for more than fifty years. As a child, he and his mother moved into a small house on Warner Avenue. Although he had moved from just one town over, he was startled to see how the Polish people on his new block lived.

He remembers the neighbors standing in their front lawns, yelling down the street to one another, walking in and out of each other's houses, going to parties at night, and stumbling home at six o'clock the morning after.

He tells me how the town has changed, and that there are no longer bars on every street corner. He squints as he tries to recall memories. This is when he starts talking about race.

"Oh, there was one black family that lived a couple blocks over. I think their son played football or something." He continues, "There were a couple Jewish kids in my grade, too." He claims that he only recently learned what "Jewish" means. In fact, he chuckles when he tells me how high school was simply a time for him to run around town rewiring telephone poles to cheat cable companies of free channels.

"It's no longer a wild town." He shrugs his shoulders. "It's boring. But for the most part, the people are really great."

**MY DAD WAS WASHING DISHES** one night, aimlessly peering out the window, when he overheard our new neighbors, an older couple, talking. He chuckled when he heard the husband say that North Tonawanda is "going to the dogs."

The couple radiated a pitiful rage. They did not care that my family originated outside the United States, or that we had spent time traveling the world. They didn't know anything about my parents' education, or jobs. Their only concern was that they were forced to live next to a black family.

That was when we first moved in, and four years later, I have yet to interact with them. According to a website run by sociologist and historian James Loewen, in New York State alone there were thirty-six suspected "sundown towns." This nickname refers to towns where black people were not welcome after sunset, and where they were prevented from living through strict housing ordinances and, in some cases, open violence. A sign stating "Nigger, Don't Let the Sun Go Down on You in [name of town]" could often be found on the outskirts of these places. Communities with a history of being sundown towns exist across the United States, especially in the Midwest. But Loewen's list includes places in New York State, like Amherst, Orchard Park, and—surprise—North Tonawanda.

These communities were predominantly white with very few minority households, and I am unsure whether inhabitants think things should be different now. I want to be optimistic, but I sometimes imagine this history still prevents people from integrating fully.

Although towns are no longer legally segregated, all-white towns still exist. And for some historic sundown towns, racial divides still seem present.

This means that my favorite secluded side roads, which intersect with the bike path along the Niagara River, near the house that I live in, are in the center of a town where no "Negro" could live from the late 1800s to the mid 1900s.

**MY MOTHER ASKS,** "How far are you going to run today?"

"Depends on how I feel. I should be back within half an hour, maybe an hour," I respond.

"Has your dinner digested properly?" My mother's voice beats into my back. "Do you have your phone on you?"

"I don't have anywhere to put it."

My dad interjects, "What if you need me to pick you up?"

"I won't," I say, as I start my watch. My mom stands in the doorway as I run down the driveway.

"Run a couple miles for me!" she cries.

Later, returning to the pavement of my driveway, legs burning, lungs heaving, and sweat dripping down my back, I am safe. I have made it. The door is unlocked, and my parents are waiting for me at the kitchen table.

"That was fast," my mom chirps. "How far did you go?"

"Only five miles," I reply.

"How was it?" she asks.

I shrug as I reach in the fridge for water. "Same old scene."

The river was quiet. I passed a few strangers. They are always older than I am. Most people my age are finishing their second drink right around this time. But some strangers say hello. Some even smile. And then there are others who do not acknowledge my presence.

I imagine that some people gawk while I run because I am young, and actively taking responsibility over my health. I assume that others gape because I am black, and uncommon.

# Solutions

# CAN'T WE ALL JUST GET ALONG?

## A Road Trip with My Trump-Loving Cousin

### Bryan Mealer

Somewhere around Fort Worth, we have our first argument in the car. Frances says something crude about immigrants, which I let pass, then she brings up Franklin Roosevelt. This is a game we play. I tell her my favorite president was FDR, then she says something like, "He was okay, except for all the handouts he gave."

Which is when I remind her of 1936. After her father died and her mother disappeared, FDR's relief checks kept her and her siblings alive.

"Yeah," she says, "but we were just kids."

"And welfare still helps kids today, along with single women like your mother."

"But it's different now," she says. "People just don't wanna work."

And when I remind her again that a majority of welfare recipients are employed, she waves me off.

"My favorite president was Ike," she says, which I know. Frances is quick to praise men she sees as having backbone—her father, Ike, Ronald Reagan, Donald Trump—and deplores whiners and eggheads. That morning, she couldn't find Fox News in her hotel room and had to settle for "some puny guy" on another network. I'm shocked when she tells me Barack Obama was "cute."

"Hated him as president, but I could watch him run up and down those stairs all day long," she says. "But Lincoln—boy, I really hate him."

I'd never heard this before. I nearly swerve out of my lane. "Lincoln? Who hates Abraham Lincoln?"

"He stood on that platform and watched those boys kill each other," she says. She's referring to the Battle of Fort Stevens in July 1864.[1] Confederate troops came within striking distance of the Capitol. Lincoln watched from an earthen parapet and was nearly shot by a rebel sniper. The first time she referenced it, I had to look it up.

"But Lincoln ended slavery," I say. "Can we agree that slavery was bad?"

"That's not why they were fighting, and you know it," she says.

I turn on some music, and try to make time.

It started as a joke.

My cousin Frances, who's ninety-three, loves Donald Trump. She's adored him ever since the beginning, from the fateful escalator ride at Trump Tower to Billy Bush and beyond. The morning after he won, when I was hungover and she called to gloat, we had some words, and didn't talk for weeks. Afterward, we vowed never to let politics get in the way of our friendship.

Then a few months ago, after the umpteenth controversy to come out of the White House, I asked her what she thought of Trump now.

"What do I think?" she said. "I like him even more. In fact, I'd drive clear to Washington just to shake his hand."

"Then I'll drive you myself," I said, kidding. "We'll go together."

But suddenly it was no longer a joke, and here we are, driving two thousand miles to try to meet the man. I assure myself that he's a germaphobe, and won't shake my hand anyway.

We began our journey in Big Spring, Texas, where Frances and I were raised, fifty years apart. I met her only three years ago, while researching my latest book, *The Kings of Big Spring*, about my family's troubled history there.

She was living in Scottsdale, Arizona—unbeknownst to us. Her father, Bud, had died of dust pneumonia during the Depression. Her mother then suffered a mental breakdown and abandoned them, leaving Frances to care for her brothers and sister. Throughout the reporting we became close, even after she discovered I was "one of them," meaning a Democrat. Most of our phone conversations took place with Fox News rumbling in the background.

I know the real work of this road trip lies in the journey itself. Along the way I've arranged to meet with people who challenge us ideologically, who represent our frustrations and tears. From our siloes of social media and cable news, we scream and rant about these enemies, yet rarely ever talk to them. And this lost civil discourse only benefits those in power.

If exposure is the antiseptic to bigotry, I want to give our stereotypes and preconceptions a proper airing.

The devil's working on you, kiddo.

## MOORE, OKLAHOMA

My plan is to get a blessing from different clergy along the way. And since we're in the most heavily evangelical state in America, I look up Pastor Mark Fuller at Abundant Life Church. He greets us in his office, which is decorated with American flags and a framed copy of the Declaration of Independence.

I like the pastor. I grew up in evangelical and Pentecostal churches, so I find him warmly familiar. Over coffee I tell him what Frances and I are doing, how we're trying to address the division in our country. He says that most of his congregation supports Trump, but during the previous administration, a few Obama supporters got angry when others insulted the president and Fuller had to intervene.

"We have to be more mature as Christians whether we agree or disagree with the current administration," he says. He quotes 1 Peter 2:17, which ends with, "Fear God. Honor the emperor." It's a quote I've been hearing a lot lately, mainly from white evangelicals when challenged about morally supporting this president.

"Well, we certainly applied that scripture when Obama was president," he tells me. "Here was a guy who was completely away from Christian ideology. Pro-abortion. Of course, pro-homosexual, pro-LGBT. So that scripture came to my attention. We have to honor the emperor and pray for them."

"That's hard," I say, searching my brain for counter-scripture, which never comes when I need it.

"It sure was!" Frances pipes in. "But you deal with it and don't riot in the street! You go to the polls and hope for the best."

I share with him my frustration about the evangelical embrace of Trump, how I find it hypocritical and discrediting, and how as a fellow Christian, it's impossible to honor a man whose actions and behavior are a direct affront to the gospel of Jesus. I tell him about my church in Austin where many in the congregation are gay and transgender, having come there after feeling ostracized in mainline churches.

These are my friends, I tell him. Our children play together. The religious right's well-tailored message that Christians can't be progressive or gay or Democrat is one I find maddening and offensive.

The pastor politely waits for me to finish, then says, "When you say welcoming LGBT, we do welcome them as well. We've had members who are inclined to that persuasion. And we welcome them with open arms. Just as anyone else involved in any other sin, we don't condemn them."

I was waiting for the "greater sinner" response, the belief that gay people are second-class citizens of the Kingdom, and when it comes my face flushes with rage. I want to grab him by the collar and shout, God made them this way, don't you people get it? But I'm stopped by the very point he was trying to make. That love is patient. Love is not easily provoked. For lack of a better argument, God and the pastor had the upper hand.

"There are differences in feelings of what is sin and what is not sin," he says, sensing my anger.

"That is indeed our difference, Pastor," I say.

We talk some more and finish our coffee, then we get up to leave. But before we go, I ask the pastor if he'll bless our journey. We form a circle in his office, hold hands, and pray.

As we enter the hills of western Missouri, Frances tells me something else I'd never heard. That after divorcing her husband Tommy, who cheated on her and sometimes hit her, she started dating a really nice guy and they became close. "But the next thing you know he's telling me he's a cross-dresser," she says. "And he married a lesbian. He's a girl now. So don't tell me about lesbians and homosexuals. I know about homosexuals."

I don't say anything.

"It just shocked me, is all," she says. "I don't know what to think when people start talking about that stuff."

"I understand," I say.

She stares out the window at the rows of dogwood in bloom, then says. "I've never been on anything like this before."

"Me either," I tell her. "It's a new experience for us both."

## FERGUSON, MISSOURI

If there was ever a polarizing force for the current divide, it's the Black Lives Matter movement. To the conservative right, the "BLMs," as Frances calls them, are the new Black Panthers, the cop-hating boogeymen of failed liberal cities driven by antiwhite rage. If Donald Trump is what's saving America, the BLMs and other ingrates who march in the streets are what's destroying it.

So I thought it was only appropriate that we visit Ferguson, where the Black Lives Matter movement began.

A couple of weeks earlier, I'd sent a Facebook message to Mike Brown Sr., whose son Michael, eighteen, was killed by police in August 2014, sparking a national outrage over violent policing in black communities. I told Mike about Frances and her love for Trump, then asked if he'd like to meet her. Since it usually falls on black activists to reach out and be understood, he was intrigued. He agreed to join us for lunch.

We meet at Cathy's Kitchen, a popular soul food place located on South Florissant, two miles from where his son's body lay facedown in the street for four hours. The riots and protests that ensued lasted for months.

Mike is tall and beefy, and still wears his signature long beard. He looks around the room before walking over, uneasy, and I realize he's more nervous than Frances. He brings his wife, Cal, whom he married two months before his son's death. The two of them now run the Michael Brown Chosen for Change Foundation, which works with youth to advocate for better policing. Just the day before, as Frances and I were discussing what had happened in Ferguson, she uttered something I found painfully old-fashioned: "Used to be," she said, "black policemen worked their own neighborhoods, and people were happy."

After introductions, I ask Mike about the foundation. He says they've been working on building bridges with the police, gaining back the trust, and vice versa. "They need to put police who live in these communities back out to police them," Mike says.

Frances puffs her chest. "I like this guy."

Cal looks at Frances. "Can I ask you a question? What do you like about Trump?"

"I think he's good for the country."

"Is it the business aspect of it?" Mike asks. "Because he's a good businessman, I agree with that. What is it?"

"I think he just loves the people."

Mike and Cal look at each other. "Everybody have their own opinion," Mike says. "You entitled to that."

"I'm just sorry to hear about your son," Frances tells him.

"Yeah. I'm still recovering from that."

"You're coping," Cal says. "You never recover."

Cal and I volunteer to go fetch drinks for everyone. As we walk away, I suddenly worry about leaving Mike and Frances alone. My recorder catches what follows:

Long silence, then Frances says, "I like sun tea."

"What's that?" Mike asks.

"You put the tea out in the yard and it makes it real good."

"Oh yeah? I'll tell my wife about that. She makes a lot of lemonade from scratch. I should've brought you some."

Over catfish and shrimp and grits, we talk about "Mike-Mike" (as Michael Jr. was called) and the day he was killed, how Mike had just gotten off work and Cal was folding laundry when someone burst open the door shouting their son was dead on Canfield Drive, about the riots that followed, the trauma and depression, and the power of good therapy. And we discussed their strange new role as grief ambassadors of Black sons killed by police. Over the past four years they've attended numerous funerals and memorials across the country, mostly of kids who didn't get the same press coverage as Mike-Mike. "When these people memorialize their children year after year, it's like sitting in the funeral all over again," Cal says. "We had to take a break. There's only so much my heart can take."

I ask what I think is the obvious question, about their role in Black

Lives Matter and what it means to see the movement take on such force. They raise their eyebrows.

"We do not like them people," Cal says.

"I don't deal with them," says Mike.

"They hijacked the movement," says Cal. "They just do their own thing."

Mike says he's met BLM representatives from other states who he did like. "But the ones who kicked this off here? Nah."

And thus, Mike Brown and Frances now have two things in common.

Later, when I ask the waitress for the check, she tells me another customer already paid it. "We get that a lot," Mike says. He asks if we have time to see something before we go. In the car, we follow him and Cal down the street to a drab, red-brick restaurant called New Chinese Gourmet. "This is where we had our last real conversation before he died," Mike says. He points through the window to a round table where all the family had gathered: himself, Mike-Mike, Cal, and Mike-Mike's sisters. Although it was summer, it was the day Mike-Mike finally completed his credits and graduated from high school. His mood was buoyant, soaring.

"He told us one day he was gonna change the world," Mike recalls, smiling. "'One day everyone gonna know my name!' Said he was gonna be a big rapper and artist, bigger than Tupac, Lil Wayne, and Biggie. He never knew he was gonna change the world in a different type of way."

"Eight days later he lost his life," Cal says. "Two days before he was supposed to walk into a college classroom. This is the first time we've been back here since that day. First time we ever even talked about it."

Frances gives them both hugs and we say our good-byes. "God sees us all the same," she says, once we're alone and driving. "Nobody deserves to lose their child."

## DUBLIN, OHIO

If there's ever a group that understands the need to reach out—to be seen as fully human by the other side—it's American Muslims. A few weeks earlier, I'd contacted Imran Malik, outreach coordinator at the Noor Islamic Cultural Center outside of Columbus, and told him about our journey. Since interfaith relations is one of Noor's biggest priorities, he'd arranged for us a welcoming party.

With more than five thousand members, Noor is one of the biggest mosques in the United States. Thinking Frances would balk at the idea of a visit, I didn't tell her until we were deep into Oklahoma and it was too late for her to bail. Her reaction surprised me. "I'll talk to anyone," she said, crossing her arms. She was out to prove me wrong.

Although it was built in the immediate wake of the September 11, 2001, attacks, the mosque started receiving threats in 2014. The phone calls, hate mail, and protest alerts continued well into Trump's candidacy. Now there's armed security for Friday prayers and the doors are kept locked throughout the day.

In a large conference room past the ornate prayer hall we're greeted by a group of men, women, and children. The women wear brightly colored headscarves, while one man wears a long robe and a skullcap. Frances is sporting her pink Ivanka.

Sitting in a circle, Frances and I explain what we're doing. Then each person says their name, their country of origin—Pakistan, Gambia, Syria—and what message they'd like to send to the president.

Halfway through, the man in the skullcap asks Frances to explain her support. "How did you choose Trump?" he asks, but what he's really asking, I sense, and what each person in this room is wondering, is how on earth can you love a man who referred to Syrian refugees as snakes, talked about shutting down mosques, pushed bogus polls saying a quarter of Muslim Americans wanted jihad, riled up crowds with fictional stories about bullets dipped in pig blood, a man who routinely negates the American experience of millions of its citizens?

Surrounded, and without breaking a sweat, Frances launches into her defense. "I don't know how I wouldn't choose him," she says. "I think he loves the people. I think he took this on because he loves the people and wants to get the country straightened out, to bring back jobs. He's very intelligent, I've read all of his books. . . ."

The group just stares at her as she talks, and in that moment, I find myself feeling oddly proud of her, not because of her answers, but because of her steel nerve. At ninety-three, she doesn't give a flip.

After that, I expect the gloves to come off, especially after a teacher named Lila tells Frances she's never felt more disenfranchised in her own country, and how she feels like Trump couldn't care less when it comes to making minorities feel welcome.

Frances tells her, "Well, he's not giving a pity party."

But the gloves don't come off. In fact, our Muslim hosts do the opposite. They listen, and then they embrace her. One woman points out how they both value faith and family. Another compliments Frances's complexion. After we finish, they surround Frances for hugs and photos, and then we all hold hands in a circle and pray. When I finally manage to pull her out of there, she's holding a gift box of assorted baklava.

Weeks later, back home, I'll read a story from 2015 about how the same congregation responded to an anti-Islam protester. Instead of ignoring the woman, the members of Noor came outside and greeted her one after another, whittled her down with humor and reason, and took the air out of the monster. Finally, one woman simply walked up and wrapped her in a hug. "I felt her body go from tense to soft," the woman wrote on Facebook, "and I asked her to please come inside with me." Which she did.

That night as I help Frances settle in to her room, she tells me what a wonderful time she had. "Weren't they the nicest people?" she says. "I made so many new friends." I agree that it was wonderful, then leave her to watch Fox News. We're not changing the world here, I think, but the next time Sean Hannity or Laura Ingraham disparages one of her new friends, I hope she'll remember the baklava.

## CHARLESTON, WEST VIRGINIA

By the time we arrive in Charleston, it's well past dark. Frances is sick, having come down with a cold, and is flagging. But I've heard there's a group of high school kids from rural West Virginia headed to D.C. for the March for Our Lives.

I know how Frances feels about protesters, but I'm curious to meet country people who are willing to march against guns.

"They probably grew up hunting," I tell her, assuming they were like us.

Upon arriving, we discover that most of the students are Black. I sense Frances deflate. Another group of haters, she's probably thinking. Simply getting her in the door had been hard enough.

The kids are from Logan, about sixty miles south. We form a circle and they start telling us how drugs have taken over their town, how it's hard to find a good job, and that people are suffering. Most of them come from low-income families. Someone had started a GoFundMe campaign to pay for their trip to Washington.

Like most American kids, they're terrified by the school shootings. And they're afraid of teachers carrying guns, because in their school, students often overrun the faculty. I then ask if they have a message for the president. If I were poor and black and stuck in Logan, I imagine I'd have plenty of angry words for Donald Trump. But that's just me projecting. These kids show way more compassion. They actually want Trump to succeed.

"Mr. Trump, we're your future," says Kiana Minter, seventeen. "Don't you want to be proud of us? You can teach us. Watch what we're doing. If we're messing up, just tell us. We're not here to make trouble."

"Try to be the best," says Tiana Sherman, sixteen. "Strive to be better than the rest of the presidents."

At every stop, people surprise us. Frances lights up in their presence. She and the girls exchange phone numbers and pose for selfies. "Never in a million years would I have met those people," she says.

The next morning, driving through a blizzard, we pull into a gas station on the way to Charlottesville. Standing in line is a man openly carrying a pistol. We start to talk. His name is Mike Welch, a former soldier who served in Iraq. On his phone he shows us video of guys battling door-to-door in the Sadr City section of Baghdad. "That's my unit," he says.

We ask Welch what he thinks about the march in Washington, which is happening as we speak—500,000 people advocating for gun reform. He answers by lifting his shirt to better display his holstered handgun. Frances laughs. I roll my eyes. Guys like this are why I don't go to gun ranges any more.

"Obviously, I'm for gun rights," Welch says.

"Yeah," I say.

"But there are things that can be done. I don't fall in line with the NRA's views as much as some of the nut jobs out here. Get real."

"Okay."

"Having to be twenty-one to own a gun isn't against the Second Amendment," he continues. He's also in favor of stronger background checks. In fact, he says, there was a longer delay than usual when buying the pistol he's carrying now. "I didn't cry like a baby because I didn't get it five minutes after I applied for it."

## WASHINGTON, D.C.

It's Palm Sunday when we enter Washington. At the gates of the White House, the usual crowd has gathered. A preacher rails against abortion. A man holds a banner against a potential war with Korea. There are students and tourists and vendors selling #MAGA hats and flags.

In one way or another, we're all here to lay our hopes and grievances at the seat of American power, or to gawk at the spectacle it has become. And inside sits the man, fresh from the green at Mar-a-Lago, whom we've driven two thousand miles to see.

In several hours, Stormy Daniels will appear on *60 Minutes* and the clouds will roll over Pennsylvania Avenue once again.

In the end, we of course never met the president—or came even close. I catch a plane back to my liberal enclave in Austin, while Frances returns to Scottsdale.

Over the coming weeks, she'll talk about missing the road and the friends we met, and how she's been writing letters. She still loves Trump, especially when he tweets, but that doesn't mean the journey was in vain. Before leaving Washington, I took her to the beauty shop, and while waiting in the next room, I overheard her describe the trip as her "crowning achievement." No longer was the country so small or frightening. Whether or not she changed her mind, she'll always have those memories and the indisputable joy they bring.

As for me, I'll wrestle over the coming days with what we experienced, still feeling frustrated by some of the encounters. But the following Sunday, on Easter, I'm in church listening to the old resurrection story when something happens.

It's a tale I've heard my entire life, ever since I was a kid, but that morning it takes on newer and greater meaning, then spreads itself into all my dark places.

Resurrection is a force that lives on within us, my pastor says. Resurrection begins with you; you are the healing of the nation. My frustration and anxiety fall away, and I realize that the journey into the divide has only begun.

# WHAT IT TOOK TO FINALLY CONFRONT MY FAMILY ABOUT RACE AND POLITICS

### Sarah Menkedick

My four-year-old daughter has recently started to notice skin color. "Mommy," she points out when we take a shower, "your skin is white, and my skin is brown, and Papi's skin is brown!" With a four-year-old's mania for classification, she lines up our arms in order of deepening darkness. She counts: "Two browns, and one white!"

The other day in the car when I said a curse word, she asked me why, and I said it was because Donald Trump was taking children away from their mothers at the border. "Why?" she asked. I tried to distill immigration down to a child's logic: "Because where they live is not safe. So they come here to have a safer life. But some people get mad that they come here. They don't want them here."

"And he takes their kids away?"

"Yes."

"Why?"

Her lip trembled. I once made the mistake of reading a library book about a hippo that lost its mother and she cried so hard I finally had to bust out a hidden stash of M&Ms.

I reiterated that some people don't want these families here, and want to punish them. She did what she does with any situation that is incomprehensible: she just kept asking why, assuming there has to be an explanation that will make sense to her. Finally I said, "Because they have brown skin, like you and Papi. Donald Trump doesn't like brown skin."

"He doesn't like brown skin?" she asked. I nodded.

"He doesn't like me?" she asked.

"Well, no," I said. Then, "Yes. But not you specifically. Just people like you. It's not because you're bad. It's because they don't like brown skin. You're not bad. This is why it's important to stand up for these other families."

Her gaze was unflinching. I was flailing; my back hurt from arching around to look at her.

"It is very important to love people no matter what color their skin is," I told her. "To be a good person. And to be proud of your brown skin."

I KNEW EXPLAINING RACE to my Mexican American child was inevitable, and I knew that I'd fumble through it. What I did not expect was how acutely I would come to feel my whiteness.

I grew up in Columbus, Ohio, in a culture of extreme whiteness. There was only one black student at my high school; I knew no Latinos.

In college, my experience was not all that different, although my first real boyfriend was a black man whose father was from Ghana and whose mother was African American. On a trip we took together in Italy, I drank half a bottle of vodka, tripped, and smashed my face onto a stone plaza.

Both of my lips were torn open and several teeth were knocked out. When we got to the emergency room, the doctors shoved my boyfriend outside, barring him from entry, insisting he'd abused me, making mock punches to get their point across.

I didn't have the words to explain and they didn't want to listen, so I sat for hours bleeding alone on a stretcher while he roamed the streets. We laughed about it on the way back to France, while I threw up every twenty minutes out the window, suffering the excesses of the night before. When we flew together, we'd conduct a little experiment: I would take all of our bags and breeze through security, and then he'd take all of our bags and every one of them would be inspected.

I should have known then about whiteness as a honeyed protective coating, one that would shield me but that could be lethal for everyone else. But in the way of so much of clueless youth, it was largely a game.

And then in 2006, in Oaxaca, Mexico, I met the man who would become my husband; in 2010, we married and moved to the United States.

Jorge, too, had grown up in a highly homogeneous community in Oaxaca's Sierra Norte, and in his childhood rarely encountered anyone of another race or ethnicity. But whereas my homogeneity corresponded to a privilege I took for granted, his corresponded to an internalized inferiority.

He studied business administration because he did not think it was practical for a kid like him—poor, Indigenous, rural—to study photography. I studied history of science because it was interesting. He cleaned hotels and worked as a barista, getting by on rice and tortillas prepared by a señora at a corner stand, all the while taking photography workshops, applying for arts fellowships, and making a name for himself. Eventually he got a position as the darkroom manager at a prestigious museum that featured workshops with renowned international photographers.

He had no interest in coming to the United States, and was never mesmerized by my foreignness. He liked me, the fact that I was outdoorsy and slightly wild and very different from him: bold where he was shy, demanding where he was acquiescent, hungry for novelty where he was rooted in place, set on running loops around the local park while he listened to Yo-Yo Ma and sketched.

We were married in Mexico, but my parents held a small reception for family in the States. An uncle, a conservative who lives in the hyper-white, hyper-Republican suburbs of Cincinnati, asked Jorge, in rhetorical tones, if he was "happy to be in America."

Jorge, being Jorge, did not mention that, in fact, his ancestors were the Indigenous peoples of the Americas. He did not say, "No, I hate it here, the food is horrible and the culture is deadening and the people are ignorant and racist." He did not say, "What in the world does that mean?" He said, "Yes." We made chitchat about the weather and drank beer and thanked everyone for coming.

Five years later, when our daughter was one, we were at a Fourth of July party in the Columbus neighborhood where I grew up. It was a block party; people wandered onto the lawn from surrounding streets, carrying foil-wrapped American flag cakes and plastic cups of wine. I took my daughter to get some blueberries, leaving Jorge alone for a minute on the grass.

When I returned, a police officer was kneeling beside him. For a minute, I actually thought, "Oh, the police officer's chatting with Jorge!"

This is when my white shame finally showed itself: after all those years of progressive politics, in that moment, staring into the righteous eyes of that white male cop who was asking my husband what he was doing here, I got it.

The rage that bloomed in me was like nothing I'd ever felt.

Being white, I had the luxury of acting on it. The cop took one look at my white face and stood up, nodded, walked away. I followed him. "Why were you interrogating my husband?" I yelled. "Why him? Why?"

Later, we would find out that an old white man in a red polo shirt, whom I'd noticed following Jorge with his eyes from the moment we arrived, had told the cop to interrogate Jorge. Later, after we filed a complaint with the police department, the cop would clarify that he worried Jorge was homeless and thought he might have a medical problem, despite the fact that Jorge is fit and trim and clean-cut, that he was wearing a new T-shirt and J.Crew shorts and had not had a drop to drink.

**FOR YEARS,** both before and after that incident, I did not talk to my extended family about race.

While my immediate family is progressive, much of my extended family is highly conservative and tends to both doubt the existence of racial bias and sympathize with racist rhetoric about, say, the Obamas or immigration.

In 2016, most of them voted for Trump.

On the night of the election, Jorge laughed and I cried. He was utterly unsurprised. "This is your country," he shrugged. "It's always been like this."

"It's not the one I know," I insisted. But of course, it is the one I know now. Family members of mine voted for a man who campaigned denouncing Mexicans as rapists and terrorists and criminals, who used "Mexican" as a slur, and the same family members could not see how that might affect my Mexican American family. Many of them embraced the notion of "both sides" after Charlottesville.

In the year after the election, I tried not to confront them about "politics," as if politics weren't a series of decisions, from their votes all the way up to executive orders, that would reshape my life.

I didn't talk politics, and then my health care premium went up to $800 a month with a $12,000 deductible because of Republican insistence on destroying the Affordable Care Act without any alternative.

I didn't talk politics, and I saw families who looked like mine being separated at the border; a man my husband's age, with a child our daughter's age, who hanged himself in a cell when his child was taken from him.

I didn't talk politics, and a Central American mother stayed at our house, slept with the light on, and sobbed so hard at our kitchen table it seemed her whole body might break.

I didn't talk politics, and I volunteered after an immigration raid that detained 149 people in Salem, Ohio, watching a mother of five—who worked in a bacon factory producing food my extended family eats—weep while she prayed for her children.

I didn't talk politics, and one Saturday morning, as I was running in our neighborhood park in Pittsburgh, I got a call from my husband telling me not to come home: there was an active shooter at a synagogue blocks from our house.

This shooter, it would turn out, had spent countless hours online being radicalized by the same far-right rhetoric—anti-Semitic conspiracy theories, fear and demonization of immigrants and refugees—that members of my family tacitly endorse.

It is thankless to get into Facebook arguments, and painful to enter into live ones. The latter experience floods me with dread and feels, in a visceral way, antithetical and unnatural. For whenever I meet my extended family in person, I am reminded that I like them. That they are just people, after all, people who give my daughter plush dinosaurs or make corny jokes.

They support me, always, even when they don't understand what in the hell I'm doing. I could show up any night and sleep in one of their houses; I could leave my daughter with them, and they would cuddle her and feed her American Kraft Singles. At the same time, many of them sympathize with the ideology of the far right, which has made me fear for my husband's life, which has led to a sharp uptick in the number of hate groups and crimes in the United States, which has inspired a massacre in my neighborhood.

The idea isn't to attack, demonize, or shame them—as Brené Brown has pointed out, shame is not a productive emotion. It makes people shut down rather than open up. But I have lived for too long in the cognitive dissonance of writing senators and representatives and marching and tweeting and Facebooking without ever actually talking to the people who perpetuate what I am fighting against.

On the left, in progressive urban areas, we have policed each other's rhetoric for the subtlest infractions and slip-ups and called each other out relentlessly for ironies or privilege without really contending with the fact that a sizable percentage of the country is okay with caging brown children and justifying white nationalism.

We condemn this without engaging with it, while it becomes clear that the rhetoric of the far right is acceptable, refreshing even, to a disturbingly significant swath of the country.

A FEW DAYS AFTER the massacre at Tree of Life in Pittsburgh, I heard an interview on *All Things Considered* with the Emory University religion professor Deborah Lipstadt. She pointed out that there had been a 50 percent increase in anti-Semitic incidents in the past two years in the United States.

The host asked Lipstadt what people could do to combat anti-Semitism, and the single most important thing Lipstadt noted was speaking out against racist comments. She said: "You know, Thanksgiving is coming up, and we all have a curmudgeon uncle who may make some comment. And people around the table, you know, say, oh, that's Uncle John, and they let it pass. We can't do that. We may not get, you know, Uncle John to change his views, but silence in the face of bigotry is acquiescence."

I reached that point last June, when my husband, daughter, and I went to the Families Belong Together march in Washington, D.C. It was hot. By 10 a.m. my daughter was covered in sweat and begging to go home, and I was *that* mom, that indie-film-character-of-the-activist-mom, saying, "There are little children who don't have their mommies who are suffering, so you can sit here on the grass and eat your apple!" She held out.

Sometime before the speeches started, I was interviewed by Fox News. I was holding Elena and sweating and she was burying her pouty face in my chest and sweating.

In the interview, I said I was horrified by what was happening since I have a daughter with roots in Latin America. On the drive back from D.C. later that afternoon, I got my first hate mail. Trolls on Twitter attacked me for all the usual reasons. And then I got a Facebook message from my aunt.

"We saw you on Fox News!" she said. "You were very eloquent and spoke well." It was a very sweet message and very much in the white nice tradition, and finally, I saw my chance.

I did not rage or blame. Instead, I told her what that protest meant to me. I told her I had helped immigrants who had been detained in a massive raid on a factory in Ohio. I told her what I'd seen there. I told her about Jorge's family, about how with just a few different circumstances he might have been climbing the border wall at night with Elena in his arms. I told her about the migrant women who've stayed at our house after being released from Eloy, in Arizona, and how they sleep with the lights on, how their children were taken from them screaming in the middle of the night.

I told her, "I am telling you this out of love, as a godchild." That was true. She used to feed me Cheez-Its and tall glasses of whole milk when I spent the night at her house. She read my book and sent me a letter afterward praising me for my bravery.

It felt awful to write that message. I was sick to my stomach afterward. I thought, *Okay, maybe that's the end of that*. But she wrote back and thanked me for telling her a story beyond the fear-driven media narratives.

I sent her an article that came out in the *New York Times* about the work Jorge and I have been doing and she read it. This feels like progress.

It is not about politics. It is about saying, "This is my life, and this is what I care about." *I care about immigrants. Here are some of their stories.* It might be the same with any other issue: *I care about health care. Let me tell you what I have suffered.* Or: *I care about abortion. Let me tell you the decision I had to make.*

This is not politics. This is us: who we are, what we believe in, who we love.

At a candlelit vigil in Pittsburgh shortly after zero tolerance was enacted, when the ProPublica tape of children sobbing and begging for their parents had just gone viral, a Black Lives Matter activist chastised all the white people in the church. "This is easy," she told us, and it was. It felt really good to be in a room full of like-minded righteous people, mostly white. The real work, she said, is exhausting. It isn't just the Instagram post of a postcard to a senator. It isn't just the rant over beers with a friend. It is a thorny, painstaking conversation with an aunt who lives thousands of miles away, remembering how she took care of you, remembering how she sends you the twenty-five-dollar gift card every year on your birthday, remembering her humanity, and then trying to show her the humanity of the people you love.

Raging at people "on the other side" in anger and righteousness is not likely to disrupt the cycle of hate; I can see this clearly. But being silent is not kind. It just hurts someone else.

Last weekend, I listened to the poet laureate Tracy K. Smith on the *On Being* podcast. She has spent the past year traveling around the country, reading poetry and talking to people. She told host Krista Tippett that she is interested in "the way our voices sound when we dip below the decibel level of politics."

I love how this sentiment gently undermines the division between politics and life. When I talk about politics, I am my most righteous, performative self. But when I talk about my life, my fears, my love, I am a person.

This past Thursday, I saw Smith in Pittsburgh. She took to the stage and said, smiling, "Love is scary." I kept repeating this to myself all week. Many people I love are scared of difference, terrified to accept it, let it in. I am scared to talk to them, and also to love them when I feel threatened by them.

These are not equivalent reactions with equivalent consequences, but I think this can be a useful mental framework for moving past my own fear, deeper into love and its responsibilities. The scary kind of love doesn't ignore difference. It sees it, moves closer to it, and engages.

# THE COOLEST PARENTS IN JOHNSON COUNTY, KANSAS

## C. J. Janovy

**W**endy Budetti had been to Costco. She'd hauled a thousand hot dogs in the back of her minivan, and now the big day was here, a sunny, sweaty Sunday at the end of June. Budetti, her husband, Brett Hoedl, and a handful of other volunteers had secured the largest sheltered pavilion in a big-city park, procured a public address system, picked up countless of bags of chips people had dropped off at the local Democratic Party office, and wondered who would show up to the first LGBTQ picnic in Johnson County, Kansas.

At the entrance to the pavilion, six-foot-tall rainbow-colored balloons spelled out the word "PRIDE." Soon their congresswoman—a Native American lesbian named Sharice Davids—was mobbed by selfie seekers after her speech to hundreds of people hunkered down at the long picnic tables and spilling out from under the shady roof and up the grassy hillside. Budetti and Hoedl could exhale and feel the day.

"Our biggest fear was that we'd throw this picnic and all of our friends would come," Hoedl says, "and that would be it." They worried they'd just see the same few dozen folks who'd been showing up lately at political events around this stereotypically conservative Kansas City suburb. By early afternoon, that fear had evaporated in the humidity.

Kansas City has pride celebrations, but in recent years those have been booze-soaked, ten-dollars-at-the-gate festivals across town on the Missouri side of the state line that divides this sprawling metro of two million people. It had been a long time since the city had seen a proper pride parade, much less a free picnic.

Early in the afternoon, a young couple decked out in glitter makeup and rainbow-colored clothes approached Budetti to tell her how happy they were. They'd never been to a pride event. "They made me cry," Budetti says. Later, as Budetti was cleaning up, a woman introduced herself as the aunt of a middle schooler who'd just come out. "We were so excited that we could bring them here," the woman said, "and show our support and love for them."

**THE FAMILY PARTY** they threw for several hundred strangers came almost three years after what Budetti describes as one of the worst parenting nights of her life.

Budetti and Hoedl had never been politically active. They'd kept up on the news, but as parents of five kids, they were busy like everyone else. The whole family, however, was caught up in progressive enthusiasm when Bernie Sanders swept the Kansas Democratic caucuses in March 2016. Whatever disappointment they felt when Hillary Clinton claimed the nomination was outweighed by the awfulness of Donald Trump.

On November 8, they took their oldest daughter to vote for the first time. Their eleven-year-old son had recently told them he was gay. That night, they settled in at their large, comfortable suburban home to watch an LGBTQ-supportive woman win the presidency. As the darkness deepened, Budetti knew she should say something to her kids about what they were witnessing. But she just went upstairs to bed. Her children were crying, but she couldn't face them.

"There was nothing we could say, like, 'Oh, it's going to be okay.' We knew that only works at a surface level."

Luckily, their actions since then have more than made up for any lack of comforting words.

Looking for ways to get more involved, one day they went to a social justice fair at a community college. There they met a gay man named Tom Alonzo, who volunteered for Equality Kansas, an LGBTQ rights organization with chapters in nearly a dozen cities and towns. Alonzo had been quietly working on a tactic other activists around the country had deployed for decades: asking local governments to pass ordinances protecting LGBTQ people from discrimination in employment, housing, and public accommodations. Since the 1970s, a few hundred cities around the country, and twenty-one states, have added these protections.

Trying to pass these laws can get ugly. Supporters frequently end up debating opponents over months of hours-long city council meetings, while media coverage forces a city's residents to think about things they'd rather not, such as the sex lives of some of their neighbors or how other neighbors use biblical justifications to say shockingly cruel things about their fellow human beings. Alonzo had stayed under the radar as he'd shepherded such an ordinance up through the bureaucratic process in Wyandotte County—the scrappier, working-class, diverse, and Democratic-leaning county north of where Hoedl and Budetti lived, in wealthier Republican Johnson County.

Activists had daunting experience with this type of effort in three other Kansas towns. The state's oldest such ordinance was in Lawrence, home to the University of Kansas, where city commissioners had banned discrimination based on sexual orientation in 1995, though they didn't add gender identity until 2011. An hour west in Manhattan, where Kansas State University rests amid the gorgeous rolling-prairie Flint Hills, activists had tried twice to pass an ordinance. A 2006 proposal died in the city's human relations committee. Five years later, after all the usual controversy, activists claimed victory when commissioners passed an ordinance on a 3–2 vote—but municipal elections two months later reversed the friendly majority, and new commissioners repealed the ordinance before it could ever take effect. The members of the Flint Hills Human Rights Project were resilient, though, and five years later they went back to city hall a third time. By August 2016, they'd succeeded.

The only other Kansas town to have passed an ordinance was in Johnson County. With only about seven thousand people, the shady and quiet community of Roeland Park might have seemed an odd place to start a fight, but members of Equality Kansas had looked at voter rolls and determined that the demographics and the time were right. They'd figured if Roeland Park passed an ordinance, Johnson County's larger cities would be inspired (or shamed) into doing so as well. After several months of agony, their strategy worked. Since 2014, however, no other town in the county had followed Roeland Park's example.

Activists who mount these campaigns know it will be wrenching but productive. If they win, they'll have made life safer for LGBTQ residents. If they lose, the months of media coverage will have educated countless people; they'll have made new friends and identified opponents and laid the groundwork for future progress. And they'll have created a community. So when Wyandotte County commissioners put Alonzo's nondiscrimination ordinance on their agenda in June 2018, the members of Equality Kansas braced for battle. Commissioners didn't even bother debating it. Instead, they just passed it. Unanimously.

Alonzo was stunned. Hoedl and Budetti figured if Wyandotte County could do it, so could Johnson County. But there were big differences between the two places. Wyandotte has a consolidated government representing about 165,000 people. Johnson is the most populated county in the state, with more than half a million people living in seventeen municipalities—the smallest town has a population of 195; the biggest city is a hundred times that size.

Budetti and Hoedl set out on an all-consuming political journey.

**JOHNSON COUNTY'S SUBURBS** ripple to the west and south of Kansas City, its oldest cities filled with postwar ranch homes while, from outer-ring freeways, glass office towers and taupe cul-de-sacs resemble the affluent outskirts of any Midwestern metro. Hoedl and Budetti came from what they describe as "completely different worlds twenty minutes apart."

Like his parents, grandparents, great-grandparents, and maybe a generation before that, Hoedl was born and raised in Olathe, where he attended a relatively diverse, working-class high school. Budetti's family was a more recent arrival to Overland Park, where she went to a mostly white school. The two met in a church youth group when they were sophomores, and by the end of their junior year, Budetti was pregnant. They married at nineteen, and the next decade brought those five kids. Budetti homeschooled them and took them to dance classes and theater rehearsals while Hoedl worked in IT at a big engineering firm. Each kid grew into their own kind of activist. Alyssa, the oldest, graduated from college with a political science degree and has interned and worked on campaigns for state representatives. Lauri, the second, helped lead her high school's student walkout to protest gun violence. Gavin, the third, knocked on an astounding number of doors for candidates before graduating high school a semester early and heading to the state capitol for his own internship with a state rep. Lizzie, the youngest, has written postcards and stuffed envelopes for candidates and deployed an ingenious subversive tactic of her own. The manager of her middle school basketball team, Lizzie kept getting rides home from different parents. Budetti offered to pick her up, but she declined. "The more people who give me rides home," she told her mom, "the more parents see our yard signs."

Their second-to-youngest, Eli, was just eleven when they noticed his sensitive response to the Instagram post of an older boy from dance classes who'd come out. One night not long after, he texted them from his bedroom: "I'm gay." They wrote back: "Please come to our room."

"We talked," Hoedl remembers, "and he knew he was in a much safer position than a lot of other kids."

Hoedl and Budetti entered the world of LGBTQ activism not because they were worried about Eli—he's secure in who he is and has never had any trouble at his high school, where he's on the varsity drill team with twenty-one girls—but because so many other kids had no support. And they weren't the only ones motivated by the 2016 election.

Over the next two years, national attention and resources poured into Kansas's 3rd Congressional District, where Sharice Davids won a crowded Democratic primary and knocked out a four-term Republican by 10 points in November 2018. That same energy elected the first two openly gay members of the Kansas House of Representatives. Fired-up Johnson County residents had also been working with Equality Kansas to propose a nondiscrimination ordinance in Prairie Village where, after two months of predictable debate, the city council passed it in December. Two nights later, Mission did the same. Merriam passed an ordinance in January, followed by Mission Woods in March and Westwood Hills in May.

It was an extraordinary thing to witness, a chain reaction of citizens refuting the stereotype of Kansas as a conservative backwater. In some cities it was easier than others, but Hoedl was always there, hanging back as the chair of Metro Kansas City's Equality Kansas chapter while people who lived in each town stood at microphones in council chambers and made their arguments.

"It's just amazing to have my dad, like, drop me off at dance and drive to whatever city's passing an ordinance and have that be almost normal," Eli says of his family's weekly routine.

Leawood and Shawnee passed ordinances in August. In October, so did Overland Park, Lenexa, and Westwood. In November: Fairway.

"It's given communities power," Hoedl says. "It makes people realize when you rally behind something that's right, you do get it done."

Except where they actually lived.

Hoedl had first approached Olathe leaders about an ordinance in January 2017. It took two years for the human relations committee to send a draft to the council, where it languished. There's nothing sexy about municipal government, but so many LGBTQ people and their supporters were showing up every first and third Tuesday to pressure council members that one activist described Olathe City Council meetings as "the new gay nightlife hot spot."

Opponents showed up, too, testifying about how they didn't hate LGBTQ people but didn't believe laws should protect them, or about how LGBTQ people are deviant and abhorrent. About how equal rights for LGBTQ people meant their own religious freedom was under attack.

"It's so hard," Budetti says, "when you hear people wrap their words in what they refer to as love: 'We love you but.' I think about these people's nephews, nieces, grandchildren, and what those kids' lives are like. That's heartbreaking to me."

Eventually it looked as if they had enough supporters on the council if only the mayor would put it on the agenda. Then came city elections in November 2019. One potential yes vote lost to a challenger from the religious right, so a 4–3 majority in their favor would soon be a 4–3 majority against them. In December, before the new council took over, the ordinance was on the agenda. The councilman who'd just lost his seat spoke passionately about why he would vote yes. Among his reasons: "This body is a secular body; it is not a church."

The moment was beautiful and infuriating. "Where were you six months ago?" Budetti whispered to no one in particular in the back of the room, where a standing-room-only crowd had waited for hours while the council slogged through a tedious list of zoning changes. Budetti and Hoedl had worked on Olathe for nearly three years, seeing ordinances pass in so many cities other than their own. She wept and hugged three of her kids—Eli, Gavin, and Alyssa—and several of her neighbors.

There was no guarantee the protections would last. The new council might repeal the ordinance like the one in Manhattan had done a few years earlier. As the Trump era was demonstrating, backlashes can be brutal. But Hoedl and Budetti and their fellow activists had brought nearly half a million Kansans on a journey toward tangible progress.

Soon, Budetti announced she was running for the Kansas Senate. She was challenging one of that body's most far-right legislators—and the apathy and complacency she still sees all around her. She bristles over the way people compliment her after hearing Hoedl on the local NPR station. "They say, 'It's great that you're doing this,' not 'How can I help?' Like, we're not here to be your entertainment. Join us in the fight, you know?" The stakes are high, she notes. "It's a scary world to be in right now."

But Hoedl and Budetti seem fearless. They've spoken at council meetings where open-carry enthusiasts have made their presence felt. City residents give their addresses when they testify. Hoedl's been on TV. His picture's been in the paper. But he says he hasn't felt afraid.

"Maybe the only time something crossed my mind was the first time we walked in the Old Settlers Parade," he says of an enormous procession that's part of a three-day, 120-year-old frontier festival every September.

Equality Kansas was marching, carrying the organization's banner in front of tens of thousands of people. "There were a lot of kids with us and they were scared," he says. They were prepared for "the absolute worst"—which isn't surprising, since active shooter drills are a regular part of school.

Instead, at points all along the route, people stood up and cheered.

# THE STRUGGLE
# OF DEATH, HOPE,
# AND HARM REDUCTION
# IN THE MIDWEST

## Zachary Siegel

F or those of us who are suffering, how do we find joy and experience pleasure? How do we create a world in which less suffering is
possible? What does it look like to build community in the face of
such suffering, and how can we create communities that are safe
for each and every person?

These are the questions that Sarah Ziegenhorn, the thirty-year-old
executive director of the Iowa Harm Reduction Coalition and a medical
student at the University of Iowa, had in mind when she and her team
organized the fourth annual Iowa Harm Reduction Summit. It took place
October 3–5, 2019, in Iowa City in the name of Andy Beeler, who died
in his home from an accidental heroin overdose in March. Beeler was a
program coordinator at the Iowa Harm Reduction Coalition, beloved by
the participants to whom he dedicated his life.

Far from an abstraction, the questions raised by Ziegenhorn were present throughout the weekend. Deaths involving synthetic opioids like illicit fentanyl tripled from 2011 to 2017, while those involving heroin quadrupled from 2012 to 2017, according to the Centers for Disease Control and Prevention. In 2017, stimulants like methamphetamine contributed to 28 percent of the 342 overdose deaths in Iowa, according to Iowa's Department of Public Health.[1] A mix of heroin, illicit fentanyl, and meth is contributing to an upswing in morbidity and mortality across the plains of Iowa and the Midwest at large.

A much-anticipated Saturday night presidential candidate forum was postponed after Senator Bernie Sanders—who was slated to wax on health care, drug policy, and criminal justice reform—had a heart attack. "Due to Senator Sanders' illness, we are postponing tomorrow evening's kick-off candidate forum," Ziegenhorn wrote in an email to panelists and speakers from out of town. "Because many of you arranged travel plans to Iowa around this event, we are throwing a party instead."

Grim statistics—and the big heart of America's leading socialist giving out—did not diminish the spirited, vulnerable tone of the weekend. Hundreds of people showed up with all the urgency that Ziegenhorn's questions express.

At many harm reduction conferences, people tend to fly in from the usual hubs: New York, Chicago, Los Angeles, Seattle, and the Bay Area. While these harm reduction hot spots were well represented in Iowa, sharing decades of wisdom and up-and-coming programs, the substance of the summit was distinctly Midwestern. Many Iowans directly impacted by chaotic drug use and inhumane policies drove hours to hear about how to expand services that save lives, and learn about innovative strategies to mitigate harms to people who use drugs and to sex workers.

## DRUG USER ORGANIZING IN A RED STATE

Topics ranged from "Eliminating Hepatitis C in Iowa: Building Financial Sustainability for Payers and Providers" to "Drug User Organizing." In the latter meeting, led by activists Jess Tilley and Louise Vincent, nearly forty people who identified themselves as drug users sat in a circle and engaged with the difficult task of how to organize in their communities and fight to be treated with dignity by medical, legal, and other institutions.

Christopher Abert, former executive director of the Indiana Recovery Alliance and founder of Southwest Recovery Alliance, told *Filter* how inspiring this had felt. "So many people identified as using drugs," he said. "I've never seen anything like that before." Indeed, they were mostly strangers to one another, but Abert felt a unique vulnerability and openness.

Tilley, who smiles with her eyes and frequently calls herself "jaded," shared with the group how safe she felt there, and then got down to the business of people who use drugs engaging in direct action against punitive drug laws. Tilley and Vincent used their Reframe the Blame campaign, which targets cruel and misplaced drug-induced homicide laws, as an example of how people can make their voices heard.[2]

Having flown in from Chicago, where harm reduction groups like the Chicago Recovery Alliance have a twenty-five-year history, I had a question on my mind beyond those Ziegenhorn raised.

In the rural Hawkeye State—which President Trump carried by the largest margin of any Republican candidate since Ronald Reagan in 1980, and where conservatives maintain a trifecta of control over the House, Senate, and governor's office—are harm reduction services, like naloxone and syringe distribution, fentanyl test strips, and support for sex workers, *really* being embraced?

The answer, I learned, is an unsatisfying *yes and no*. But groups like the Iowa Harm Reduction Coalition are moving the needle. Part of this involves building bridges with critical institutions at the university and the state's criminal-legal system.

## A TROUBLED RELATIONSHIP WITH RELIGION

An exchange during one of the weekend's most moving workshops illustrated the moral and political complexity of providing harm reduction services in deep-red political terrain and within conservative institutions.

Early Saturday morning, Blyth Barnow, of Faith in Public Life, had delivered what was by all accounts a fiery sermon on bridging the gap between harm reduction and the Christian church.

"As a community organizer, I knew that better understanding the language and values of Christianity could be a powerful tool when attempting to make change somewhere like Ohio," Barnow said with the force of a preacher. "But perhaps most importantly, I wanted to learn how to bury my friends with dignity, because nobody else ever had."

When Barnow's ex-boyfriend died from an overdose fifteen years ago, she was livid in the aftermath.

"I lost one of my first loves to an accidental overdose on heroin and crack," she said. "He came from a family of evangelical Christians, and at his funeral all his friends who had been caring for him sat in the back of the church while his family, who I trust loved him in some way, but who also kicked him out and called him an abomination, got to sit up front."

The pastor at the funeral condemned him to Hell for his sins.

"In theory it would be easy to say 'fuck the church' and walk away," said Barnow. "It is harder to admit that that day, the pastor reaffirmed what many of us already felt—that we were worthless, we were broken, we were dirty, and that we ought to be ashamed of ourselves. I sat in a row of about ten of my friends that day, and almost all of them are dead or locked up now."

She continued, "In our society, clergy are granted authority and power. His words had the power to turn our self-criticism into a truth.

It created so much harm. And I truly believe that hearing that message from a pulpit was part of what cost my friends their life and their freedom. When left unchecked, toxic theology kills people. Which is why we need to get and stay in the mix."

Ever since she graduated from seminary, Barnow and others, like Rev. M. Barclay and Erica Poellot, director of faith and community partnerships at the Harm Reduction Coalition, have been pushing religious communities to embrace harm reduction. Connecting biblical concepts like resurrection to lifesaving drugs like naloxone, the overdose antidote, Barnow has organized church services called "Naloxone Saves," at which naloxone kits are blessed on the altar.[3]

"It was harm reduction that taught me that resurrection is possible," Barnow told the room. "Harm reductionists are some of the most powerful ministers I know, whether they want to claim that title or not."

After Rev. M. Barclay, Barnow, and Poellot took turns speaking, Ziegenhorn shared how local church communities in Iowa shut the Iowa Harm Reduction Coalition out, refusing to give them space to store syringes and naloxone. Ziegenhorn said her team sent emails to local churches about the faith and harm reduction workshop, and in terms of those local churches, "nobody fucking showed up!"

Barnow, Poellot and Rev. Meg Wagner, of the Episcopal Diocese of Iowa, shared Ziegenhorn's frustration and told her to not give up. It will take time and patience, they said, to engage with traditionally conservative institutions about harm reduction concepts.

But with powerful synthetic fentanyl analogues taking over the heroin market, spreading across the Midwest from the East Coast, time is an unaffordable luxury.

The Iowa Harm Reduction Summit was instituted four years ago as a series of talks and panels to teach medical students how to better care for people who use drugs in their community. Today the coalition constitutes Iowa's largest free naloxone distribution program and provider of opioid overdose prevention education, and the summit attracted hundreds of people.

Beeler, who was thirty when he died, was Ziegenhorn's partner. A generation of people from all kinds of backgrounds and professions has grown up in a world of unfathomable grief. Yet even if harm reduction concepts are not being embraced by conservative legislators in red states (nor even by liberal politicians in big cities), this generation is fighting to create a world where people don't have to grow up losing so many loved ones.

Hundreds of attendees at this year's summit were among those who have suffered. They're simply fighting so that they and their loved ones, year by year, can suffer a little less.

# CONNECTING IN THE HEARTLAND

## By Paul DeMain

My family comes from part of the heartland, of the northern heartland.

My Ojibwe/Oneida/Scottish history resides in the middle of this continent. We are from Wisconsin. Even more, the center of the northern half of the Western Hemisphere can be found in the middle of our state at Poniatowski.

We have rolling forests of maple, oak, and pine, and an abundance of lakes with wild rice and varieties of fish. Where I live, on the Lac Courte Oreilles Reservation, we are four or five hours from Madison and Milwaukee, and only an hour to the largest Great Lake to the north, called Gitchi-Gumi in Ojibwe. We have a huge musky replica in town that contains a walk-in museum and we hold North American's largest cross-country ski race, the American Birkebeiner, right into our downtown. We love our Green Bay Packers, Wisconsin cheese, and—at least for me—my treaty venison from the basin of Lake Superior (the Great Lakes Ojibwe have a treaty reserved right to hunt).

I moved here in 1977 to work as the editor of the tribal journal, and I've lived here ever since, with the exception of four years when I had a second residence near the state capital, where I served as a policy advisor on tribal issues to Governor Anthony S. Earl. I returned in 1986 to start *News from Indian Country*, an independent Native newspaper covering Indian Country across the United States and Canada.

This land is also home to second- and third-generation immigrants— Germans, Polish, Italians, and Finns—and there's lots of ancient Indigenous experience to behold. We are sometimes ahead of the social curve, and sometimes behind. The true middle.

Some nearby waters flow north into Lake Superior, and onward east into the Atlantic Ocean. Others flow south, a part of the massive Mississippi watershed. Our Ojibwe elders used to tease that we might float to the Gulf of Mexico if we had the time.

In 2001, *News from Indian Country* moved into their newly designed office building. At the time, the company was publishing not only our own paper, but the *Gaming Guide*, the *Pow Wow Directory*, and *Akiing*, a regional publication for local Indigenous people. With seventeen employees and more than fifty contributing photographers, writers, and graphic designers, we had everything from breaking national news, obituaries, and sports coverage to op-ed pages. We investigated crimes, chronicled the birth of Indian gaming, and reported on conflicts over tribal treaty rights.

Outside, passersby would drive into our parking lot and sit in their cars. Unexpectedly, we had become a trading post—one that you didn't need to go inside. They were logging on to the internet, often late into the night, engines running.

I'd heard that the same thing had happened around newly installed internet hot spots on the expansive Navajo Reservation in the southwest. Clusters of cars would sit outside a chapter house parking lot, some fully loaded with heads bent over, looking at laptops or, eventually, phones.

As the only hot spot in the area, we'd become a virtual community center. Eventually we decided to just invite everyone inside.

We served gourmet coffee and provided a place for local artisans to put their work on consignment sale. We offered books, music, and Indigenous food products from wild rice to white flint hominy corn. You could visit the shop and engage in the local political banter or just catch up with one of your cousins. There was a hub of activity both in and outside the place.

We were part of the dawning of the digital age. But this wasn't our first foray.

Our company, which eventually included the trading post and an expansion into television, had worked closely with the University of Wisconsin to train Native students in new media. We were the first, in the early 1980s, to get one of those powerful MacIntosh 128k computers, replacing our Compugraphic, a pagination machine for newspapers. It was clear: this computerizing of processes made our lives so much easier. I could almost see the four-day workweek coming.

A decade (or more) later, the 2000 Nader presidential campaign asked for our help. The campaign went on to break everybody's perception of what a campaign could accomplish, including getting the coolest-looking campaign phone you could then find: *the bag*.

The bag was a "portable phone" provided by the campaign. You know, the exact thing you used to find on the wall, a handset you picked up, then dialed, attached to a brick-sized portable battery and stored in a huge black bag.

It was wondrous. I grew up with a rotary phone on the wall, and a shared line with three other households. Back then you didn't worry about upload or download speeds or connectivity. You worried about how long the conversation was going to last and whether you could get the line before some other neighbor.

You could now drive or walk around with your phone bag hanging by your side while you enjoyed a latte. The heartland was going high tech.

Better yet, grab your computer for a table conversation and log in to your latest email account. While you were plugging in, might as well try out the latest trends in "Expresso" drinks, or the daily special. Pretty tough rez life around here!

As we now age, we talk about those "good ole days," a day when you called a friend from the bag and got through to another one on the Pine Ridge Reservation—but only if you parked by the local dump to get reception. I knew exactly where my friends at Pine Ridge were when they called me on the weekend. We connected whenever they were willing to drive to a high bluff to catch a signal from the distant towers of Rapid City.

Soon, only a few elders will remember these ancient technical advancements.

Despite our learning HTML, Web management, multiple platforms, applications, and all the social media stuff that moves our economy, the internet has been both a boon and a bust to us.

Our newspaper, like many others around the country, lost out. We have instant news, instant feedback. You no longer need a store of any kind when you can order everything from the comfort of your home or office.

We have since ended publication of *News from Indian Country* and all of its affiliates. We were one of many who could not adapt to changing times, though you can't say we didn't try. A couple years earlier we closed the Trading Post as well. The ability to order your music by the tune rather than the disc, and shop from the comfort of your home, stressed our sales. The times were changing.

Luckily now, I have fourteen grandchildren to help guide me through the maze of technical apps and settings. The simplicity of the bag is gone. Now the phone sits in your pocket and delivers notification after notification that somebody, somewhere also wants your immediate attention.

# WHERE IS TRUMP COUNTRY?

## Oakley Fugate

'm from Hazard County, Kentucky, but I'm not from Trump Country. Trump Country doesn't exist. It is only used to strengthen tired stereotypes of an entire region, to equate one perspective with millions of perspectives. But it's a common phrase, even here, and the media gets a free pass because they have always demonized this region, stereotyped us since before my dad was born.

But, no, Trump Country doesn't exist. It's a kind of disease that infects the nation. On a recent trip to New York, someone I met was shocked that I was wearing Converse. That's the power of stereotype.

Decades and decades of mistrust in politicians gives Trump his appeal here, because he's not a real politician. People here are sick of career politicians and wealthy people who have too much influence and who keep the state red. And many are sick of people like Mitch McConnell, one of the wealthiest senators in the country, from one of its poorest states. As in the saying, "the enemy of my enemy is my friend," people supported Trump because they believed his promise to boost the economy, to bring back coal. He was the only candidate who promised that—the left said coal would be dead.

And many remain unconvinced because they hear a Democratic candidate saying he will take their AR-15. They hear that and think it's a step toward taking all of their guns.

*Those dumb hillbillies don't need guns like that!* is what they hear.

But many commentators don't understand why people would cling to their guns. It's because in the not-distant past, coal companies had so much wealth that they would buy off the police, and unarmed protesters were murdered. So what happens when you can't trust the police? You will arm yourself, and a lot of people in Kentucky live in the hollers where police are hours away, if you're lucky.

And so when someone comes along who says he'll bring back coal (even if he can't), who says he'll let folks keep their guns, who angers career politicians (the same ones who are now sucking up to him), people kind of get behind the guy. People here aren't dumb—they are just tired.

It is so easy to demonize someone for voting for someone who stands for everything you're against. Indeed, I found myself confused by his cultlike following. But insulting them, angering them, telling them that they deserve to lose their job and health care because of the guy, isn't going to win them over. It's only going to make people who are on the fence stick to their guns.

I worry because the Democratic Party has mastered the art of shooting themselves in the foot. I worry because there is no one running who really understands this region. I worry because there is no vision from the left that includes people like me.

And I worry because when Governor Matt Bevin was voted out, the media ran with that. We are taking back "Trump Country," in a way. Never mind the fact that only 35 percent of eligible voters actually voted, and Bevin, despite being despised here, despite demonizing teachers and doctors, two very large employers in the region, lost by only 5,000 votes, and he was able to get a recount. It was that close. It is always that close.

[*Editor's Note: Fugate, a documentary filmmaker, interviewed a few of his neighbors to ask them what they think when they hear the term "Trump Country" as part of his ongoing work to document the diversity of his community. These are the transcriptions.*]

## VENUS OCTAVIAN, AGE EIGHTEEN, PRESTONSBURG, KENTUCKY

**Fugate:** What do you think of when you hear the term "Trump Country"?

**Venus:** My nose wrinkles. [laughter] I think a lot of the reason that Appalachia is so red in voting is because of voter suppression. A lot of people that are registered Republican have a decent amount of money. So they have reliable transportation. They have the means and resources to be able to get out and vote. Whereas, a lot of the people registered Democrat don't necessarily come from that rich background, and so a lot of these people don't have the means to get out and vote. Voting is on a working-day during working hours, and so a lot of people have to choose between voting or an eight-hour payday. For a lot of people that voting window isn't necessarily something that they can achieve.

Trump Country means voter suppression for me. It also means that we are seen by the more liberal states as ignorant. This was true beforehand, but it's especially true now because there's also an uprising happening in Appalachia that is visible. And when people see that they say, "Oh, you're the ones that voted for this person. You're the ones that voted him into office."

But the thing is, the people that are leading this rebellion, the people that are fighting in this fight for liberation, they're not the ones that voted. It's the people with money that voted these people in, Trump specifically.

I think that a lot of that is shown in the relationship that former governor Matt Bevin had with Trump. It showed that there's some stuff we're not aware of. Maybe that's not voter fraud, and maybe that's not whatever, but it's definitely true that the rich of Appalachia and Trump have something going on in common. It gets me really angry to think about that because of certain people and certain votes that we're all seen as these Trump-loving Americans.

## CAITLIN CUMMINGS, TWENTY-THREE, HAZARD COUNTY, KENTUCKY

Trump Country to me is . . . I really thought that people would have more sense and see the oppression that was about to happen, I mean, that's already been happening, but I think it means: scared, oppression, hatred, racism, sexism, and just bigotry in general.

I think that [Trump's election] has given the enemy the voice. By the enemy I mean white supremacy groups. You see a lot more of them being a lot more vocal about what they're doing. And it's because they have Trump, they think they finally have this voice of reason.

I think, though, that [Trump's election] has brought light to what's been going on for a while, of what America's been trying to just sweep stuff under the rug. . . . But it has made racism and hatred just so much more normalized. I feel like we were starting to make some really good steps in the right direction, then he got elected and I just feel like it's took us back so many more steps.

I think that people like Trump prey on people here in Appalachia because they think we are uneducated. Some folks are, but that's because the system's made them that way. It's just been years and years of constantly putting people in rural communities down to lift the rich back up. Forget those in poverty because the rich, they have their money and they think that's all that they need.

They want to keep us poor and uneducated. But what they don't realize, though, is that there are so many people in this area that want change and that fight for change every day. But of course those things are never brought to light because Appalachia has always been shown in a negative light when it comes to media and other things.

Appalachia has always been represented so poorly in the media. I mean, anything I've ever seen about an area that's supposed to be similar to [Appalachia], the people have always been ignorant and dirty. And that's because they're poor. That's something that's always bothered me—that poor automatically means dirty or less than.

But classism is one of the biggest issues in America. And I think people like Trump just make that so much worse because the people that can actually see the issues and actually want to do better about these issues are not always, but usually the people that are less fortunate than the people that are rich and empowered; I mean they see that it's there. I mean, I don't see how anyone couldn't see that it's there, but they choose to ignore it because I know that if they speak out and do anything about it, and then they're going to lose all that money and they're going to lose that position and power . . . or they just don't care. And they want to continue to work in that system of power and oppression just as long as they can still get that fat paycheck and they can still screw around on their wives and they can still sexually assault people and nothing ever gets done about it.

And that's what Trump Country is. We don't hold people accountable.

I really hope that in 2020, I really hope that people are more able to vote, that they're registered to vote. I myself want to do more; I'm trying to help people to vote because that's so important. Shit, but then again it's also hard because you can get these people up and ready and out to vote, but then you still have the Electoral College, which was the reason in the first place that Trump got elected.

Those are all I guess you could say about the people in the social issues, but that's not even talking about the environment and climate change, which our president does not think exists. Other countries are doing different things and experimenting with how to take care of their waste and carbon footprint and reduce it as best they can, then you have Trump who calls for new oil lines to be put in every other month and continues to push for businesses to be built that will just take away from what little earth we have left.

I think Trump really preys on people, on rural communities. I think he made those people a lot of false promises. Like he was going to bring the coal mines back and he was really going to be there for Kentucky and Appalachia. But in return, you've seen more and more coal miners are losing their jobs, not getting paid, protesting. It's crazy that companies can get away with stiffing everyone but also that protesting lost payments from the coal industry has become the norm. And I hope they continue to protest because that's what we need; we need more people to rise up against these systems of oppression. These systems aren't built for us. They're built for the rich and the wealthy and the powerful. We need more people to rise up and realize that that system wasn't built for them, and that we have to work together to make better systems that are built for us and built for our people.

# REPORTING FOR AMERICA

## Maggie Messitt

In January 2019, just days before Florida's governor accepted the state legislature's recommendation to formally apologize to four black men accused of raping a young white woman seventy years earlier, the *Orlando Sentinel* asked its readers for absolution.

Three of the accused were arrested in 1949: Samuel Shepherd, Walter Irvin, and Charles Greenlee. A cartoon on the front page of the *Sentinel* depicted four empty electric chairs with the caption, "No Compromise!" Within days the fourth accused, Ernest Thomas, was shot by a group of men in a manhunt. Similar mobs started to burn the homes of black residents.

"The story had many more ugly twists and turns marked by lies, cover-ups and injustice. You wouldn't know it from reading the *Orlando [Morning] Sentinel* in the years immediately following the incident," the editorial board confesses.

The *Sentinel*'s coverage enflamed a racist narrative and tainted the ability for a fair trial in the local courts. This fact was even cited in the 1951 Supreme Court decision overturning the convictions of Shepherd and Irvin based on the unconstitutional exclusion of black residents from the jury.

Later that year, Shepherd and Irvin were being transported from prison to jail by the Lake County sheriff and both men were shot on an isolated back road. The only witness was the sheriff who shot them, claiming they were trying to escape. Shepherd died. Irvin survived and claimed the sheriff had instructed them to get out of the vehicle and then tried to assassinate them.

Soon after, the *Sentinel* published an editorial in absolute support of the sheriff, asserting "we have no doubt he was telling the truth" about shooting in self-defense.

Twenty-one years later, the sheriff who killed Shepherd would be removed from office as he was indicted for the murder of another black prisoner.

Irvin was retried and imprisoned until his release in 1968. Greenlee was released in 1962. But, in 2012, after all four men had passed, an FBI investigation revealed that the 1949 medical examinations of their accuser showed no evidence of an assault. It would take another seven years for the newspaper to admit its role in the men's convictions.

"Today," the *Sentinel*'s editorial closes, "we ask the public's pardon for a period when our coverage fell short."

The *Sentinel*'s admission of guilt is not a first.

In 2000, the *Jackson Sun* in Tennessee published a series of articles on the civil rights movement and created an online resource that chronicled events throughout Jackson in the 1950s and '60s—an attempt to cover today what wasn't covered then.

In 2004, the *Lexington Herald-Leader* in Kentucky apologized for its failure to adequately cover the civil rights movement. At the time that the movement was changing the country, the newspaper's management operated under the principle that, the less coverage they gave the movement, the quicker it would go away. Until the 2004 apology and the special insert published alongside it, images and reportage about protests in Lexington and sit-ins across the city had rarely, if ever, been published by the city's local paper.

In 2006, the *Charlotte Observer* and the *News & Observer* in North Carolina both apologized for their roles in the Wilmington Race Riots of 1898. "We apologize to the black citizens and their descendants whose rights and interests we disregarded," the *Observer* wrote, "and to all North Carolinians, whose trust we betrayed by our failure to fairly report the news and stand firm against injustice." Each paper's editorial ran alongside a jointly produced sixteen-page special report titled "A Painful Past," chronicling events that led to the riots and anti-black activities, including efforts by local newspapers to support white supremacists and seek the removal of antisegregationists from office.

And, just two days before Obama's inauguration in 2008, the *Meridian Star,* a daily paper that covers eastern Mississippi and western Alabama, apologized for its past coverage of civil rights issues.

These were not isolated failures.

The history of U.S. journalism is largely a history of neglecting and even harming disenfranchised communities—black communities, immigrant communities, Native communities, poor white communities.

In the 1930s, as coal mines across West Virginia closed and the state's unemployment rate reached 80 percent, the workers who remained were trapped in deep poverty and scrip-dominated economies. White supremacy was on the rise across the country, as was anti-immigrant rhetoric. But issues affecting rural, company-created communities like these were often ignored by local and national newspapers both. The companies did their best to keep the conditions of their workers out of the papers, and the papers obliged.

In the span of five years, beginning in 1930, it's believed that nearly eight hundred men died of silicosis in what remains the worst industrial disaster in American history—West Virginia's Hawk's Nest Disaster. Tunnel workers slowly died from toxic levels of silica dust caused by the company's mandated drilling practices, which focused on speed over safety. Three miles of silica dust choked black and white workers alike, many of whom were outsiders in West Virginia, lured from other states during the Depression.

It took six years for this slow-motion disaster to garner media attention, and only because of congressional hearings seeking to classify silicosis as an occupational disease. The disaster is nearly entirely absent from newspaper archives of the times and was edited out of West Virginia's edition of the WPA state guidebook series before its publication. The best documentation of the industrial disaster is in *The Book of the Dead*, a poetry collection.

In 2018, reporter and West Virginia native Molly Born moved to Williamson in the heart of the state's southern coalfields. From her apartment above a laundromat on a mostly abandoned main street, she sought to cover communities that had long lacked representation in the state's newspapers and on the public radio station. Molly had moved there to report for West Virginia Public Broadcasting, leaving a higher-paying reporting position at the *Pittsburgh Post-Gazette*. She had to navigate deep-seated distrust from residents across the region she covered—who couldn't believe that a reporter would come to live alongside them at all.

Just north of her, Caity Coyne joined the *Charleston Gazette-Mail* with the same beat—address the long-standing coverage gap of the southern coalfields. The newsroom had won the Pulitzer Prize for investigative reporting one year earlier and featured several powerhouse reporters, including Ken Ward, who would be named a McArthur Genius Fellow that same year. To the west, Will Wright had moved into a trailer down by a creek in eastern Kentucky, with the aim of reopening the long-closed Pikeville Bureau for the *Lexington Herald-Leader*. He became a bureau of one covering thirteen rural counties.

Quickly, Wright learned residents of southeastern Kentucky did not trust the *Lexington Herald-Leader.* They saw journalists as outsiders, and, historically speaking, they are correct—most journalists parachute into regions like this to report a story and depart when they think they have it. They believed journalists did little more than perpetuate stereotypes. That journalists write stories *about* them, not for them.

Within his first weeks there, Wright attended a meeting that revealed a significant water crisis for residents in Martin County. The intake pump connected to the district's treatment plant had shut down due to freezing winter weather. They had a spare pump, but the district was $800,000 in debt and had no cash flow to make the necessary repairs. So they shut off the water, hoping for the natural water pressure to sort things out.

Residents were angry.

Will covered the issue closely and regularly.

His reporting put pressure on the troubled general manager of the water district, who subsequently retired, and prompted then Kentucky governor Matt Bevin and U.S. representative Hal Rogers to quickly promise $4.6 million in federal grants to help address the crumbling infrastructure. The district also approved a rate hike that would begin to chip away at their debt.

This all happened within the first few months of the year. And because of this, Wright was eventually met with "far more hospitality than distrust or resentment" as he reported on issues that mattered most to the region.

But, while Wright was reporting on the water issue, Caity Coyne was only weeks into starting at the *Charleston Gazette-Mail* when it declared bankruptcy. The paper went up for auction, secured new local owners, and then started layoffs.

The *Gazette-Mail* was not out of the woods. Like all papers in America, they'd been hit hard by advertising and subscription losses. Nationally, in 1990, more than 62 million households subscribed to newspapers. In 2018, that number was less than half of that. Between

2004 and 2018, one in five papers shuttered and closures are not steadying anytime soon.

Apologies for historical wrongs by newspapers started to rise at the beginning of the twenty-first century, potentially setting the stage for coverage that would better represent ignored communities. But the beginning of the twenty-first century also marked the accelerating impact of the digital landscape—just one of several reasons newspapers are closing across America. Today, half of the 3,140 counties in the United States have only one paper, often a resource-stripped weekly paper, leaving enormous community and issue-based coverage gaps. More than two hundred counties have lost a news source entirely. In the span of only ten years, newsroom employees across the country had been cut in half.

Born, Coyne, and Wright were part of a project called Report for America, then still in its pilot phase, a national service program seeking to address critical coverage gaps in local newsrooms across the country—a hybrid of the national service movement and traditional, boots-on-the-ground journalism.

In full disclosure, I served as the national director of Report for America in its first two years and know these narratives intimately. In their first year, each of these journalists forged new paths for their newsroom, building trust in communities by showing up and sticking around. By listening. And by seeking to increase their cultural competency of place—by developing deep connections that lead to deeper stories.

Together, throughout 2018, these reporters and their newsrooms worked together to increase coverage of water issues in eastern Kentucky and southern West Virginia. They stayed focused on the neglected infrastructure that played a huge part in unsafe drinking water, pushing each state to address these on behalf of local residents. They held the powerful accountable. Their series of print and audio reportage, called "Stirring the Waters," prompted immediate action by lawmakers and state regulators. The Kentucky Public Service Commission initiated a study to determine how much of the water that passes through treatment plants gets lost in leaky pipes and meters before it ever reaches customers. The Kentucky attorney general called for a state takeover of the Martin County water district and resolutions passed through the state house and senate to create a task force to study what policy changes were needed to safeguard customers and prevent the financial collapse of more of the region's crumbling water facilities. In West Virginia, lawmakers cited this reportage in their debates over the water quality act and whether or not they should adopt the EPA's recommendations to regulate ninety-three pollutants in water across the state. It was also cited in the state's $55 million plan that would eventually be approved by the EPA to address infrastructure upgrades and development in wastewater and drinking water management.

This is the fourth estate at work. As it was designed, journalism is to verify and question matters of governance and power, whether that's public or commercial. Facts are not connected to morality. Facts are not connected to ideology. Facts are not connected to politics. Together, the work of these journalists illustrates the power and importance of addressing critical coverage gaps through local journalism. Not just gaps that have been created by the slow dissolution of newsrooms, but also coverage gaps that existed long before, because of historical decisions to ignore the concerns of the less powerful.

A few months after these three joined Appalachian newsrooms, more Report for America reporters were placed in newsrooms seeking to address these historical coverage gaps. More were added in 2019. Even more in 2020.

Manny Ramos and Carlos Ballesteros joined the *Chicago Sun-Times* soon after its new owners established their commitment to the working-class residents of Chicago. Both journalists grew up in Chicago and the neighborhoods they've been tasked to cover: the south and west sides. Until then, the only real coverage of these communities focused on crime. To move forward, newspaper leadership had to recognize the ways in which past coverage had created a single narrative about these neighborhoods. Ramos and Ballesteros were tasked to cover these neighborhoods with a focus on telling stories unconnected to crime.

Savannah Maher, citizen of the Mashpee Wampanoag tribe, joined Wyoming Public Radio to report remotely on the Wind River Reservation and the two tribes that reside there: the Eastern Shoshone and Northern Arapaho. A second reporter, Chris Aadland, the son of an enrolled member of the Leech Lake Band of Minnesota, is also covering the Wind River Reservation, but for the *Casper Star-Tribune*. Now in their second year of reporting, they are just two of nineteen journalists across the country tasked to cover Native affairs for their local newsrooms—an unprecedented level of attention to this historic coverage gap across all news outlets in the country, supported by a training partnership between Report for America and the Native American Journalists Association.

Each of these communities require patience and time. Just placing a journalist is not enough to heal the rifts newspapers have caused—through neglect, through hostility to the concerns of the underrepresented, through privileging of the lives of the powerful over those of the powerless. These are not new wounds.

Identifying long-neglected coverage gaps, placing and supporting dedicated reporters, amplifying their stories—this alone will not fix the crisis in local journalism. It will not fix the outdated financial model still haunting newspapers. It won't solve the continued closure of newspapers themselves. But without this effort, which we are seeing inside some newsrooms, no solution for the crisis in journalism will work. Any model that solves these financial struggles must incorporate local reporters with a thoughtful focus on underserved communities and issues. Otherwise, we are just waiting for another round of apologies.

# Afterword

# ALL I COULD HEAR WAS SICKNESS

## Coronavirus from Inside a Prison

### Lamar L. Walker

I went to bed early that night. It was a Sunday, and it was oddly busy for a Sunday. The institution had moved ten inmates around to other parts of the prison, causing a slight panic. I've been incarcerated for over thirty years, and I have never seen bed moves like this on a Sunday. None of us have.

The entire population here at Marion Correctional Institution had been tested just a few days before for the coronavirus. We had gotten no information about the results, so naturally, we were in speculation overdrive.

"The people they moved were infected," I heard someone say. That was the first notice—and it ran in a constant loop in my head.

My neighbor was one of the guys moved. He slept three feet away from me.

He'd been lying in his bunk moaning for the past six days, and I kept telling him to go talk to a nurse.

I was afraid that he could have infected me. I'd felt a rush of dizziness and disorientation a couple of times that day, so I decided to lie down. Sleep seemed like the only escape from a constant diet of COVID-19 panic. By 7:30 p.m., I was out.

**THE FIRST TIME** I ever laid my head on a prison pillow, I was on edge, too. I was young and angry and scared, swinging at anyone who tried to get too close, anyone who looked at me sideways. I was spiraling down—that is, until I met George. He caught up with me in the rec yard one day, after I had gotten into it with some young dude. He told me I had to slow down and be less reactive, keep quiet, stand my ground. He became like a father to me, helping me to navigate prison life. He was always studying something—astronomy, ancient history, art. He read my writing and encouraged me. I told him I thought he should write a book, but he'd always laughed it off.

I don't know how long I slept, but I was sleeping hard. A sudden surge in noise throughout the room shook me awake. I scanned the dorm and noticed a few guys gaping at the television screens.

"What the hell is going on?" I asked my neighbor.

"Dawg," he said and turned to me like he'd just seen a moose run through the dorm. All I heard was cursing and hissing. No one was making any sense. I reached over and turned on my television. "They just said like 1,856 people tested positive for the damn coronavirus."

"Here?" I adjusted my eyes to the bright screen to get a look for myself.

"Yeah, here . . ."

The rolling chyron at the bottom of the screen confirmed the number: "1,856 inmates test positive for COVID-19 at Marion Correctional Institution."

"How is that even possible?" I asked.

"That ain't even all of the test results!" he yelled.

The dorm was in an uproar.

"They tryin' to kill us!" somebody yelled.

I fell back on my pillow at a loss, turned off my TV, and just listened to all the theories being thrown about.

"We all got the shit," someone yelled. That was the last thing I wanted to hear.

But it was pretty obvious that the guys they moved earlier were not the guys who tested positive for COVID-19.

"Were they the only guys that tested negative?" I asked.

"Ten guys out of four hundred?" It couldn't be. I tried my best to shut out the noise, and settled back down for sleep.

But for the rest of the night, all I heard was sickness. Two beds to my right, and one row over, someone had a nasty cough. His phlegm was rattling. I turned over, and covered my head.

One bed to my left, and one row back, maybe five feet away, one of my buddies vomited into a trash can.

All I could hear was sickness. I don't think I've ever felt so vulnerable in my life.

Social distancing is absolutely impossible in prison. I can reach to the left or right of me and literally touch my neighbor's bed. I hid underneath my blanket, tucking the sides under my legs in an attempt to block out the virus. In that makeshift cocoon, I prayed for the first time in a long time. My parole hearing had already been delayed because of the pandemic, so they let me have it by video. I had taken classes, kept my record spotless, and prepared for a year. But after fourteen years inside, I knew better than to hold too tightly to hope.

"I have grandchildren I've never met," I told God, like He didn't know. At that moment, it seemed like that was the only thing that mattered. "I can't die without meeting my grandchildren."

Masks were passed out, and the institution was locked down—two weeks too late. Visits were canceled, and mandated classes were cut down. But staff members were still conducting classes without masks or any real protection. By the time the first corrections officer died and extreme lockdown was implemented, it was a nightmare.

Now we are not allowed in our dayroom or outside on the yard. When we are called to chow, fifty guys wait in line standing maybe a foot and a half apart.

I've learned that the inmates serving food—the guys preparing the paper-sack lunch bags and passing them out to everyone else—were already infected. I watched one of the line servers get rushed out by the nurses, and all I could do was shake my head.

"They trying to kill us," I heard someone say again. The conspiracy hacks just gained a new member.

Every single individual I associate with shows symptoms. Many have lost their senses of taste and smell. For a week straight, two or three guys were being carted out by nurses every day. George could barely walk when they carried his six-foot-four frame out the door.

Today is only my second day without severe dizziness, or vomiting up the small amount of fluid I'm able to get down. I pray that the parole board releases me before the second wave of COVID-19 hits M.C.I. We're too vulnerable; we're too overcrowded.

I was just informed that George died. He had a great mind. I've never heard better metaphors or similes from anybody. I can't believe I'll never see him again. I really wish he had listened when I told him to write something.

# ACKNOWLEDGMENTS

The editors would like to thank Adam Weinberg and Raj Belani for their unwavering support of the work and mission of the Between Coasts Forum. Many thank-yous also to our colleague Margot Singer for her vision for the Narrative Journalism program at Denison as well as her ongoing support of the forums.

Thank you to the people whom we lean on the most to make the forum come to life: Beth Lossing, Ted Genoways, Mary Anne Andrei, Peter Slevin, and Kari Lydersen.

We would also like to thank Liz Stearns, Casey Grieco McNeally, Aaron Fuleki, and Sarah Schaff for all their work on BetweenCoasts.org. Special thanks to Carson Vaughan for his work on our most recent stories. Lastly, and most importantly, to our families for tolerating our "ideas" and incessant work.

Karen Coates and Valeria Fernández's story was reported with a grant from the International Women's Media Foundation. Mya Frazier would like to thank Jeremy Keehn.

Special thanks to Christopher Greathouse for his help in securing Lamar Walker's piece. Many of these pieces went through the hands of other fine editors and fact-checkers before we even saw them. For their work, we thank them as well.

# CONTRIBUTOR BIOGRAPHIES

**Sydney Boles** is a reporter for 88.7 WMMT FM, a community radio station serving eastern Kentucky and surrounding areas, in partnership with the public radio collaborative the Ohio Valley ReSource. She covers economic transitions in formerly coal-reliant communities.

**Graham Lee Brewer** is a contributing editor for Indigenous affairs at *High Country News* and a board member at the Native American Journalists Association. Brewer is a member of the Cherokee Nation. He lives in Norman, Oklahoma.

**Karen Coates** is an independent journalist, editor, and media trainer who covers food, environment, health, and human rights globally. She is a fellow with the International Women's Media Foundation (IWMF), ambassador to the Center for Environmental Journalism at the University of Colorado Boulder, and president of the Rio Grande Chapter of the Society of Professional Journalists. She is also a contributing editor for *Archaeology Magazine*. Her story in this anthology, with Valeria Fernández, originally appeared in *Pacific Standard*. It is part of a long-term project to investigate child labor in U.S. agriculture, with support from IWMF. Karen is the author of four books, and a producer/editor on the forthcoming documentary film *Eternal Harvest*.

**Courtney Crowder**, the *Des Moines Register*'s Iowa columnist, traverses the state's ninety-nine counties telling Iowans' stories. A graduate of New York University, Crowder previously worked at the *Chicago Tribune*. She's a parallel parking master acquainting herself with gravel roads. Follow her on Twitter @courtneycare.

**Paul DeMain**, also known by his Ojibwe name Skabewis, is the former editor of the now defunct national Native newspaper *News from Indian Country* published from Hayward, Wisconsin. He currently produces video for IndianCountryNews.com and continues his work with Native communities through his chairmanship at the Navajo Times Publishing Company, Honor the Earth, and as a special projects coordinator in the Great Lakes for the Inter-Tribal Agriculture Council.

For nearly two decades, multimedia journalist **Valeria Fernández** has investigated immigration in Mexico, Guatemala, and the United States. She has produced documentaries for Discovery Spanish, PBS, and CNN Español and has written for the *Guardian*, *California Sunday Magazine*, Al Jazeera, and the Associated Press. Her work on human rights abuses in Mexico against incarcerated Central American youths was featured on PRI's *The World* and NPR's Spanish podcast, *Radio Ambulante*. She teaches bilingual journalism at Arizona State University. In 2018, she received the Heising-Simons Foundation's American Mosaic Journalism Prize.

**Mya Frazier** is an investigative and business journalist based in the Midwest. A regular contributor to *Bloomberg Businessweek* magazine, she has seen her work also appear in NewYorker.com, *Outside*, *Columbia Journalism Review*, *The New Republic*, *Slate*, *The Atlantic*, *Harper's*, *Aeon*, the *New York Times*, *American Demographics*, and *Columbus Monthly*. She is a former staff writer at the *Cleveland Plain Dealer*, *Advertising Age*, and

American City Business Journals, and has twice been awarded fellowships from the McGraw Center for Business Journalism at the CUNY Graduate School of Journalism. In 2018 she was the recipient of an 11th Hour Food & Farming Fellowship from the UC Berkeley Graduate School of Journalism and an Ohio Arts Council Individual Excellence Award.

**Oakley Fugate** is a filmmaker from Whitesburg, Kentucky, who has been a part of Appalachian Media Institute at Appalshop since 2012. His work explores local issues such as LGBTQ rights, mental health awareness, and coal miner activism. Fugate's work has been featured in numerous places, including *Oxford American* and the *New York Times*. In 2017, Oakley was one of six around the country to be selected in the Open Society Foundation fellowship and opened a safe space in his hometown of Whitesburg.

**Ted Genoways**, a contributing editor at *The New Republic*, is the author of *This Blessed Earth: A Year in the Life of an American Farm* and *The Chain: Farm, Factory, and the Fate of Our Food.*

**Esther Honig** is an award-winning radio journalist currently based out of Mexico City, where she reports on agriculture, immigration, and the impacts of climate change. While working stateside, her coverage has focused on rural middle America, including Kansas, Missouri, Ohio, and Colorado. Her work has been featured by NPR news, Public Radio International, and *PBS NewsHour* among others.

**Mei-Ling Hopgood** is a journalist and the author of *Lucky Girl* and *How Eskimos Keep Their Babies Warm*. She has received several journalism awards, including the National Headliner Best in Show and ICIJ Award for Outstanding International Investigative Reporting. She teaches at the Medill School of Journalism, Media, and Integrated Marketing Communications at Northwestern University.

**C. J. Janovy**'s book *No Place Like Home: Lessons in Activism from LGBT Kansas* (University Press of Kansas, 2018) won the 2019 Stubbendieck Great Plains Distinguished Book Prize, was nominated for a Lambda Literary Award in LGBTQ nonfiction, and earned a spot on the Kansas Notable Book list of 2019. She is an editor at KCUR, Kansas City's NPR affiliate, and spent ten years as editor of the *Pitch*, Kansas City's Village Voice Media–owned alt-weekly newspaper. She and her wife have two dogs.

**Brittany King** is a graduate of the University of Missouri and is now an independent journalist based in the Midwest. She reports on education, race, and women's issues. Her work has appeared in *The Lily*, *The Indianapolis Recorder*, *Pacific Standard*, and Ebony.com.

**Bryan Mealer** is the author of *The Kings of Big Spring*, *Muck City*, and the *New York Times* bestseller *The Boy Who Harnessed the Wind*—written with William Kamkwamba—which is now a Netflix film starring Chiwetel Ejiofor. He's also the author of *All Things Must Fight to Live*, which chronicled his years covering the war in the Democratic Republic of Congo for the Associated Press and *Harper's*. His work appears regularly in the *Guardian*, and has also been published in *The New Republic*, *Texas Monthly*, and *Esquire*. Mealer and his family currently live in New York City, where he's pursuing a master's of divinity at Union Theological Seminary.

**Sarah Menkedick** is the author of *Ordinary Insanity: Fear and the Silent Crisis of Motherhood in America*, forthcoming from Pantheon in April 2020. Her first book, *Homing Instincts* (Pantheon, 2017), was long-listed for the PEN/Diamonstein-Spielvogel Award for the Art of the Essay. Her work has been published in *Harper's*, *Pacific Standard*, the *New York Times*, the *Washington Post*, the *Los Angeles Times*, the *Guardian*, Oxford

*American, Guernica,* the *Kenyon Review,* the *Paris Review Daily,* and elsewhere. She lives with her family in Pittsburgh.

**Maggie Messitt** is author of *The Rainy Season,* long-listed for the 2016 Sunday Times Alan Paton Award in South Africa, where she was a journalist, editor, and the founding director of a rural nonprofit news organization and journalism school for eight years. Messitt has edited the work of writers ranging from students to Pulitzer and Orange Prize winners, and managed editorial projects for the BBC, POV Documentary Films, Wisconsin Public Television, and others. Until recently, she was the national director of Report for America, a national service program addressing critical coverage gaps in newsrooms and communities across the country. She is currently a Mellon Fellow in Narrative Journalism at Denison University and faculty in the Creative Nonfiction MFA program at Goucher College.

**Heather Sinclair Shaw** is a writer and editor of fiction and memoir. Her writing has appeared in *Best of Ohio Short Stories* and *Vine Leaves.* She is a former Think Write Publish Science and Religion Fellow and co-founder of the Newark (Ohio) Writers Workshop.

**Zachary Siegel** is a journalist living in Chicago. His work covering public health and the criminal-legal system has appeared in *New York Times Magazine, The New Republic, The Nation,* and *The Atlantic,* among others. He is a fellow of the Health in Justice Action Lab at Northeastern University School of Law.

**Peter Slevin** is a contributing writer for *The New Yorker,* focusing on politics. He is the author of "Michelle Obama: A Life," which was a finalist for the 2016 PEN/Jacqueline Bograd Award for Biography. He is based in Chicago and teaches at Northwestern University's Medill School of Journalism.

**Wendy S. Walters** is the author of *Multiply/Divide: On the American Real and Surreal* and two books of poems.

**Fitale Wari's** writing has appeared in *Pittsburgh Post-Gazette, Between Coasts*, and *Ayyaantuu News*. She is a graduate of the Narrative Journalism program at Denison University. Wari was born in Ethiopia and raised in Buffalo, New York.

**Tamara Winfrey-Harris** is a writer who specializes in the ever-evolving space where current events, politics, and pop culture intersect with race and gender. Her work has appeared in the *New York Times, Cosmopolitan, New York, The American Prospect, Ms.*, and other media. She is the author of *The Sisters Are Alright: Changing the Broken Narrative of Black Women in America* (Berrett-Koehler 2015) and the upcoming *Letters to Black Girls*, due out in spring 2021, also from Berrett-Koehler. Learn more about Tamara at TamaraWinfreyHarris.com.

**Elliott Woods** is a correspondent at *Outside* and contributing editor at the *Virginia Quarterly Review*. He lives in Montana.

# PREVIOUSLY PUBLISHED

"The Many, Tangled American Definitions of American Socialism," Peter Slevin; a version first appeared on the NewYorker.com, June 14, 2019.

"Searching for the Other Midwestern Swing Voter," Wendy S. Walters, Zora: Medium, October 29, 2019.

"Compromised: Environmentalists, Islamophobes, and a Chicken Plant," Ted Genoways; a version of this was first published by *The New Republic*, December 6, 2017.

"The Young Hands That Feed Us," Karen Coates and Valeria Fernández, *Pacific Standard*, July 9, 2019.

"In Rural Colorado, Undocumented Immigrants Defend Themselves from Encroaching Immigration Agents," Esther Honig, is based on reporting she did for Harvest Public Media.

"Dollar General Hits a Gold Mine in Rural America," Mya Frazier, *Bloomberg Businessweek*, October 11, 2017.

"Fear: How the NRA Sells Guns in America Today," Elliott Woods; a version of this was first published by *The New Republic*, April 16, 2018.

"White Working-Class Grievance and the Black Midwesterner," Tamara Winfrey-Harris. A version of this essay, called "Stop Pretending Black Midwesterners Don't Exist," was published in the *New York Times*, June 16, 2018.

A version of "Race Home" by Fitale Wari first appeared in Between Coasts.org.

"Can't We Just All Get Along?: A Road Trip with My Trump-Loving Cousin," Bryan Mealer; a version of this was published in the *Guardian*, May 29, 2018.

"What It Took to Finally Confront My Family about Race and Politics," Sarah Menkedick, first appeared in the *Guardian*, November 21, 2018.

"The Struggle of Death, Hope, and Harm Reduction in the Midwest," Zachary Siegel; a version first appeared on Filter.org, October 7, 2019.

# NOTES

### The Many, Tangled
### American Definitions of Socialism

1. "Socialism vs. Capitalism?," Monmouth University Polling Institute, May 6, 2019, https://www.monmouth.edu/polling-institute/reports/monmouthpoll_us_050619/.

2. Mohamed Younis, "Four in 10 Americans Embrace Some Form of Socialism," Gallup.com, March 30, 2020, https://news.gallup.com/poll/257639/four-americans-embrace-form-socialism.aspx.

3. Frank Newport, "The Meaning of 'Socialism' to Americans Today," Gallup.com, March 30, 2020, https://news.gallup.com/opinion/polling-matters/243362/meaning-socialism-americans-today.aspx.

4. Peter Slevin, "Trump Asks Wisconsin to Help Elect Him Again in 2020," *New Yorker*, May 1, 2019, https://www.newyorker.com/news/dispatch/trump-asks-wisconsin-to-help-elect-him-again-in-2020.

5. "U.S. Senate: The Censure Case of Joseph McCarthy of Wisconsin (1954)," January 19, 2017, https://www.senate.gov/artandhistory/history/common/censure_cases/133Joseph_McCarthy.htm.

6. "Bay View Rolling Mill," Wisconsin Historical Society, August 8, 2017, https://www.wisconsinhistory.org/Records/Article/CS5252.

7. "Full Text of 'Building the Social Democratic Party,'" Internet Archive, n.d., https://archive.org/stream/BuildingTheSocial DemocraticParty/0000-seidel-buildingtheparty_djvu.txt.

8. "Socialism vs. Capitalism?," Monmouth University Polling Institute, May 6, 2019, https://www.monmouth.edu/polling-institute/reports/monmouthpoll_us_050619/.

## Searching for the Other Midwestern Swing Voter: (Spoiler: She's Black and Lives in Detroit)

1. "Household Composition in Metro-Detroit: Female Family Based Households Makeup Majority of Detroit," Drawing Detroit, May 6, 2013, http://www.drawingdetroit.com/household-composition-in-metro-detroit-female-family-based-households-makeup-majority-of-detroit/.

2. Bankole Thompson, "Bankole: In Defense of Black Women," *Detroit News*, September 13, 2018, https://www.detroitnews.com/story/opinion/columnists/bankole-thompson/2018/09/12/defense -black-women/1277531002/.

3. Jamie L. LaReau, "GM's Hourly Workers in Warren Speak Out Ahead of Debates, Factory Shutdown," *Detroit Free Press*, July 30, 2019, https://www.freep.com/story/money/cars/general-motors/2019/07/30/democratic-debate-gm-hourly-warren-detroit/1868916001/.

4. Antonia Noori Farzan, "A Detroit Music Festival Charged White People Double. Then the Backlash Started," *Washington Post*, July 8, 2019, https://www.washingtonpost.com/nation/2019/07/08/detroit-music-festival-charged-white-people-double-then-backlash-started/.

5. Sam Roberts, "2008 Surge in Black Voters Nearly Erased Racial Gap," *New York Times*, July 20, 2009, https://www.nytimes.com/2009/07/21/us/politics/21vote.html.

6. Jens Manuel Krogstad and Mark Hugo Lopez, "Black Voter Turnout Fell in 2016 US Election," Pew Research Center, May 12, 2017, https://www.pewresearch.org/fact-tank/2017/05/12/black-voter-turnout-fell-in-2016-even-as-a-record-number-of-americans-cast-ballots/.

7. Melanie Eversley, "Black Women Voters Will Be Central to the 2020 Presidential Election, Experts Predict," *Fortune*, June 20, 2019, https://fortune.com/2019/06/20/black-women-voters-2020-election/.

8. Andrea González-Ramírez, "DNC Appoints Three Women of Color to Senior Leadership Roles," Refinery29, April 10, 2019, https://www.refinery29.com/en-us/2019/04/229502/democratic-national-committee-new-hires-women-of-color-2020.

9. Ron Hilliard, "DNC Chair to Michigan Crowd: Black Vote 'Vital,'" WEYI, July 30, 2019, https://nbc25news.com/news/local/dnc-chair -to-michigan-crowd-black-vote-vital.

10. "4th Annual Survey 2018: Power of the Sister Vote," National Coalition on Black Civic Participation (n.d.), https://www.ncbcp.org/assets/ 2018Essence_BWR_Political_Poll_Survey_Findings9.12.18FINAL.pdf.

11. Andre M. Perry, "Black Women Are Looking Forward to the 2020 Elections," Brookings Institution, January 10, 2019, https://www .brookings.edu/research/black-women-are-looking-forward-to-the- 2020-elections/.

## Bodies on the Line:
## Protest, Politics, and Power on an Appalachian Railroad

1. Bill Estep, "Coal Jobs and Production Fell Sharply in Eastern and Western Kentucky in 2015," *Lexington Herald-Leader*, February 1, 2016, https://www.kentucky.com/news/state/article57684253.html.

2. "Table 18. Average Number of Employees by State and Mine Type, 2018 and 2017," U.S. Energy Information Administration (n.d.), https://www.eia.gov/coal/annual/pdf/table18.pdf.

## The Young Hands That Feed Us:
## An Estimated 524,000 Children Work Unimaginably
## Long Hours in America's Grueling Agricultural Fields,
## and It's All Perfectly Legal.

1. "Facts About Agricultural Workers," National Center for Farmworker Health, 2018, http://www.ncfh.org/uploads/3/8/6/8/38685499/fs -facts_about_ag_workers_2018.pdf.

2. "Working Children: Federal Injury Data and Compliance Strategies Could Be Strengthened," United States Government Accountability Office, November 2018, https://www.gao.gov/ assets/700/695209.pdf.

3. Phillip Martin, "The Costs and Benefits of a Raise for Field Workers," *New York Times*, September 30, 2011, https://www .nytimes.com/roomfordebate/2011/08/17/could-farms-survive -without-illegal-labor/the-costs-and-benefits-of-a-raise-for-field -workers.

## Fighting to Breathe:
## East Chicago's Struggle for Clean Air and Soil

1. "USS Lead Superfund Site Community Involvement Activities," Environmental Protection Agency, February 27, 2020, https://www .epa.gov/uss-lead-superfund-site/uss-lead-superfund-site-community -involvement-activities.

2. "USS Lead Sampling Data Maps," U.S. EPA Region 5 (n.d.), https://epa.maps.arcgis.com/apps/MapSeries/index.html?appid=d45 c8610b7364b8f931fdbb748d607c1.

3. "Environmental Health and Medicine Education," Centers for Disease Control and Prevention, June 12, 2017, https://www.atsdr .cdc.gov/csem/csem.asp?csem=34&po=10.

4. "ARSENIC CAS # 7440-38-2," Division of Toxicology and Environmental Medicine, Agency for Toxic Substances and Disease Registry, August 2007, https://www.epa.gov/sites/production/files/ 2014-03/documents/arsenic_toxfaqs_3v.pdf.

5. "Public Health Assessment for U.S. Smelter and Lead Refinery, Inc.," Agency for Toxic Substances and Disease Registry, January 27, 2011, https://www.atsdr.cdc.gov/hac/pha/ussmelterandleadrefinery/ ussleadphablue01272011.pdf.

6. "Blood Lead Levels in Children," Centers for Disease Control and Prevention (n.d.), https://www.cdc.gov/nceh/lead/acclpp/lead_levels _in_children_fact_sheet.pdf.

## Fear: How the NRA Sells Guns in America Today

1. Kim Parker et al., "The Demographics of Gun Ownership in the U.S.," Pew Research Center's Social & Demographic Trends Project, December 31, 2019, https://www.pewsocialtrends.org/ 2017/06/22/the-demographics-of-gun-ownership/.

## White Working-Class Grievance and the Black Midwesterner

1. "2010 Census Shows Black Population Has Highest Concentration in the South," U.S. Census Bureau, May 19, 2016, https://www

.census.gov/newsroom/releases/archives/2010_census/cb11-cn185.html.

2. "Retro Indy: African American Settlements," *Indianapolis Star*, February 9, 2015, https://www.indystar.com/story/news/history/retroindy/2015/02/09/african-american-settlements/23114613/.

3. Jeanette Lach and Joseph S. Pete, "U.S. Steel Starts Layoffs of up to 323 Workers at Gary Works," nwitimes.com, April 24, 2015, https://www.nwitimes.com/business/steel/u-s-steel-starts-layoffs-of-up-to-workers-at/article_a2368734-c52f-5ee2-8761-2b9f03734c30.html.

4. Rakesh Kochhar and Anthony Cilluffo, "How U.S. Wealth Inequality Has Changed since Great Recession," Pew Research Center, November 1, 2017, https://www.pewresearch.org/fact-tank/2017/11/01/how-wealth-inequality-has-changed-in-the-u-s-since-the-great-recession-by-race-ethnicity-and-income/.

5. Valerie Wilson, "People of Color Will Be a Majority of the American Working Class in 2032: What This Means for the Effort to Grow Wages and Reduce Inequality," Economic Policy Institute, June 9, 2016, https://www.epi.org/publication/the-changing-demographics-of-americas-working-class/.

## Race Home

1. Sarah Larimer and Cleve R. Wootson Jr., "After Blaze at Firefighter's Home, Investigators Arrest His Neighbor—a Former Firefighter," *Washington Post*, August 5, 2016, https://www.washingtonpost.com/news/morning-mix/wp/2016/08/04/a-black

-firefighter-received-a-racist-threatening-letter-then-a-suspicious
-fire/?utm_term=.d15622477bf2.

## Can't We All Just Get Along?
## A Road Trip with My Trump-Loving Cousin

1. "President Lincoln Under Fire at Fort Stevens (U.S. National
Park Service)," National Parks Service (n.d.), https://www.nps.gov/
articles/president-lincoln-under-fire-at-fort-stevens.htm.

## The Struggle of Death, Hope,
## and Harm Reduction in the Midwest

1. "Iowa Substance Abuse Brief," Iowa Department of Public Health,
December 2018, https://idph.iowa.gov/Portals/1/userfiles/133/
IASubAbuseBriefNewsletterDec2018_Final.pdf.

2. Maia Szalavitz, "These Drug Users Don't Want Their Dealer
Prosecuted if They OD," Vice, August 20, 2018, https://www.vice
.com/en_us/article/kzyk7n/these-drug-users-dont-want-their-dealer
-prosecuted-if-they-od.

3. Danae King, "Faith Leaders Told That Reversing Overdoses
among Drug Users Is an Act of Resurrection," *Columbus Dispatch*,
September 6, 2019, https://www.dispatch.com/news/20190906/
faith-leaders-told-that-reversing-overdoses-among-drug-users-is-act
-of-resurrection.